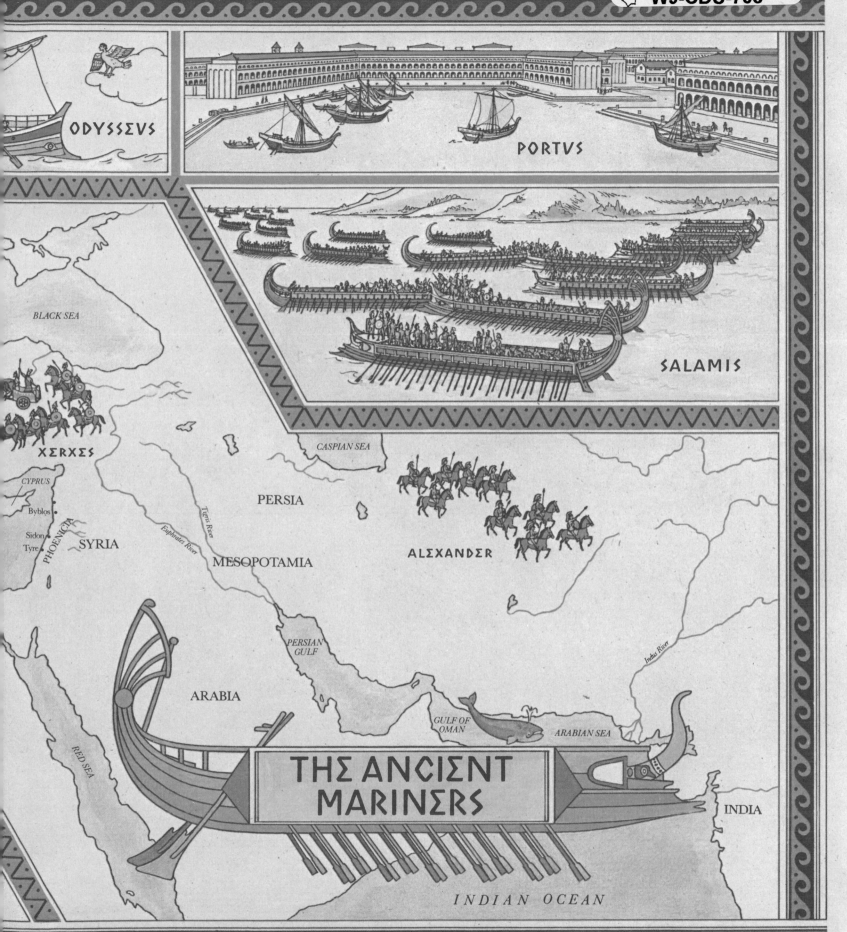

ODYSSEVS

PORTVS

SALAMIS

BLACK SEA

XERXES

CYPRUS

Byblos

Sidon

Tyre

PHOENICIA

SYRIA

CASPIAN SEA

PERSIA

Tigris River

Euphrates River

MESOPOTAMIA

ALEXANDER

PERSIAN
GULF

Indus River

ARABIA

GULF OF
OMAN

ARABIAN SEA

RED SEA

THE ANCIENT
MARINERS

INDIA

INDIAN OCEAN

The Seafarers THE ANCIENT
MARINERS

TIME
LIFE ®
BOOKS

Other Publications:

LIBRARY OF HEALTH
CLASSICS OF THE OLD WEST
THE EPIC OF FLIGHT
THE GOOD COOK
THE ENCYCLOPEDIA OF COLLECTIBLES
THE GREAT CITIES
WORLD WAR II
HOME REPAIR AND IMPROVEMENT
THE WORLD'S WILD PLACES
THE TIME-LIFE LIBRARY OF BOATING
HUMAN BEHAVIOR
THE ART OF SEWING
THE OLD WEST
THE EMERGENCE OF MAN
THE AMERICAN WILDERNESS
THE TIME-LIFE ENCYCLOPEDIA OF GARDENING
LIFE LIBRARY OF PHOTOGRAPHY
THIS FABULOUS CENTURY
FOODS OF THE WORLD
TIME-LIFE LIBRARY OF AMERICA
TIME-LIFE LIBRARY OF ART
GREAT AGES OF MAN
LIFE SCIENCE LIBRARY
THE LIFE HISTORY OF THE UNITED STATES
TIME READING PROGRAM
LIFE NATURE LIBRARY
LIFE WORLD LIBRARY
FAMILY LIBRARY:
    HOW THINGS WORK IN YOUR HOME
    THE TIME-LIFE BOOK OF THE FAMILY CAR
    THE TIME-LIFE FAMILY LEGAL GUIDE
    THE TIME-LIFE BOOK OF FAMILY FINANCE

The Cover: A Roman relief from the
First Century B.C. depicts a war galley, its
oarsmen protected by wooden walls, its
fighting deck manned by armored marines
and its bow dominated by a wooden
turret from which archers fired down on
an enemy deck. The ship is of the type
used by Cleopatra against the Romans; the
crocodile on the bow was her ensign.

The Title Page: In an engraving on
a tiny red-jasper gem, a Greek galley looses
her single sail to the wind while
the oarsmen help speed the vessel along.

The Seafarers

THE ANCIENT MARINERS

by Colin Thubron
AND THE EDITORS OF TIME-LIFE BOOKS

TIME-LIFE BOOKS, ALEXANDRIA, VIRGINIA

Time-Life Books Inc.
is a wholly owned subsidiary of

TIME INCORPORATED

FOUNDER: Henry R. Luce 1898-1967

Editor-in-Chief: Henry Anatole Grunwald
President: J. Richard Munro
Chairman of the Board: Ralph P. Davidson
Executive Vice President: Clifford J. Grum
Chairman, Executive Committee: James R. Shepley
Editorial Director: Ralph Graves
Group Vice President, Books: Joan D. Manley
Vice Chairman: Arthur Temple

TIME-LIFE BOOKS INC.

MANAGING EDITOR: Jerry Korn
Executive Editor: David Maness
Assistant Managing Editors: Dale M. Brown (planning),
George Constable, Gerry Schremp (acting), Martin Mann,
John Paul Porter
Art Director: Tom Suzuki
Chief of Research: David L. Harrison
Director of Photography: Robert G. Mason
Assistant Art Director: Arnold C. Holeywell
Assistant Chief of Research: Carolyn L. Sackett
Assistant Director of Photography: Dolores A. Littles

CHAIRMAN: John D. McSweeney
President: Carl G. Jaeger
Executive Vice Presidents: John Steven Maxwell,
David J. Walsh
Vice Presidents: George Artandi, Stephen L. Bair,
Peter G. Barnes, Nicholas Benton, John L. Canova,
Beatrice T. Dobie, Carol Flaumenhaft, James L. Mercer,
Herbert Sorkin, Paul R. Stewart

The Seafarers

The Ancient Mariners was prepared under the
supervision of Time-Life Books by the following
contributors:
Editors: Sheldon Cotler, A.B.C. Whipple
Picture Editors: Jean I. Tennant, Linda Ferrer
Chief Researcher: Cinda Siler
Assistant Designer: Leonard Vigliarolo
Researchers: Susan Sivard, Mary Hart,
Suzanne Odette Khuri
Writers: Carl Desens, Brian Dumaine, Harold C. Field,
Eileen Hughes, E. Ogden Tanner
Art Assistant: Diana Raquel Vazquez
Editorial Manager: Felice Lerner

Time-Life Books editorial staff for *The Ancient Mariners:*
Researchers: Patti H. Cass, Philip Brandt George,
W. Mark Hamilton
Art Assistant: Robert K. Herndon
Editorial Assistant: Cathy Sharpe

Editorial Production
Production Editor: Douglas B. Graham
Operations Manager: Gennaro C. Esposito,
Gordon E. Buck (assistant)
Assistant Production Editor: Feliciano Madrid
Quality Control: Robert L. Young (director), James J. Cox
(assistant), Daniel J. McSweeney, Michael G. Wight
(associates)
Art Coordinator: Anne B. Landry
Copy Staff: Susan B. Galloway (chief), Anne T. Connell,
Celia Beattie
Picture Department: Jane A. Martin
Traffic: Kimberly K. Lewis

Correspondents: Elisabeth Kraemer (Bonn);
Margot Hapgood, Dorothy Bacon, Lesley Coleman
(London); Susan Jonas, Lucy T. Voulgaris (New York);
Maria Vincenza Aloisi, Josephine du Brusle (Paris);
Ann Natanson (Rome).
Valuable assistance was provided by: Martha Mader
(Bonn); Katrina van Duyn (Copenhagen); Mirka Gondicas
(Athens); Judy Aspinall, Karin B. Pearce, Sylvia Pile, Jill
Rose, Milly Trowbridge (London); Jane Walker (Madrid);
John Dunn (Melbourne); Carolyn T. Chubet, Miriam Hsia,
Christina Lieberman (New York); Bianca Gabrielli, Mimi
Murphy (Rome); Peter Allen (Sydney); Traudl Lessing (Vienna).

The Author:
Colin Thubron, a longtime student of the
Mediterranean world, is the author of nu-
merous books on the Middle East, includ-
ing *Mirror to Damascus* and *Journey into
Cyprus.* For Time-Life Books, he has writ-
ten *Jerusalem* and *Istanbul* in the Great
Cities series and *The Venetians* in The
Seafarers series. Among his novels are *Em-
peror* and *The God in the Mountain.* A de-
scendant of John Dryden, the first English
Poet Laureate, he lives in London and is a
Fellow of the Royal Society of Literature.

The Consultants:
John Horace Parry is Gardiner Professor of
Oceanic History and Affairs at Harvard
University. British born, he served as a
commander in the Royal Navy and is a former President of the *University of Wales.*
His books include *Trade and Dominion*
and *Europe and a Wider World*—two vol-
umes about maritime exploration.

Lionel Casson is a leading authority on the
maritime history of the ancient world. His
works include *Ships and Seamanship in
the Ancient World,* and a volume titled,
like this one, *The Ancient Mariners.* He is
also author of *Ancient Egypt* in the Time-
Life Books Great Ages of Man series.

For information about any Time-Life book, please write:
Reader Information, Time-Life Books,
541 North Fairbanks Court, Chicago, Illinois 60611.

TIME-LIFE is a trademark of Time Incorporated U.S.A.

Library of Congress Cataloguing in Publication Data
Thubron, Colin, 1939-
    The ancient mariners.
    (The Seafarers)
    Bibliography: p.
    Includes index.
    1. Mediterranean region—History, Naval.   2. Naval
history, Ancient.   3. Greece—History, Naval.
    4. Rome—History, Naval.   I. Time-Life Books.
    II. Title.   III. Series: Seafarers.
DE61.N3T48   387.5'0938   80-28817
ISBN 0-8094-2740-4
ISBN 0-8094-2739-7 (lib. bdg.)
ISBN 0-8094-2738-9 (retail ed.)

Contents

Chapter 1

Traders and warriors on an uncharted sea

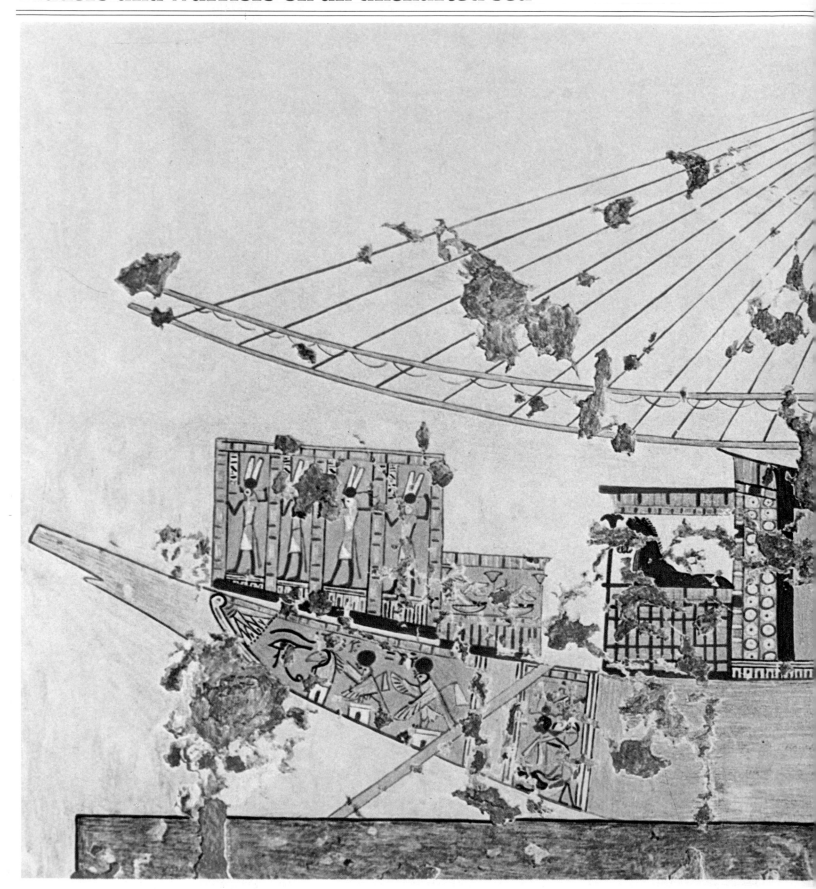

Its sail furled, an Egyptian state barge rocks at a mooring in this facsimile of a 14th Century B.C. wall painting found in a tomb at Thebes.

lmost 2,000 years before Christ, an Egyptian merchant vessel with a crew of 120 men sailed down the Red Sea, seeking a cargo of copper ore from the royal mines in the Sinai Peninsula. Such voyages were not uncommon; the significance of this one is that it ended in disaster—and yielded the earliest written record of a shipwreck.

The author is anonymous; nor does he reveal the name of his ship, saying little more than that she was 180 feet long and 60 feet in the beam. For the time, this was an immense cargo vessel, but a vulnerable one nonetheless. Then as now, the Red Sea was rent by sudden, devastating storms, and the coast provided few ports of refuge. "We flew before the wind," the mariner recalls in his papyrus journal. His description of the wreck is succinct in the extreme: "The ship went down; of all in it only I survived."

He does not say whether he rode some of the wreckage through the storm-whipped waves; he only relates that "I was cast upon an island." His first act was to find shade from the blazing sun. For three days he lay on the beach, recovering from his ordeal. Finally hunger forced him to explore his surroundings. He found "figs and vines, all kinds of fine leeks, fruit and cucumbers," and he even caught some fish and birds. Gratefully, the castaway kindled a fire "and made a burnt offering for the gods."

The journal then offers a narrative twist that, for all its improbability, was characteristic of the chronicles of ancient seafaring. The mariner claims that he was confronted by an enormous monster—"45 feet long"—which, instead of devouring him, took him to its den. The beast could even speak the sailor's language, and it informed him that a rescue ship would pick him up in four months' time. And that, says the castaway, is exactly what happened. Six months later he was home to tell his story—not only the oldest known account of a disaster at sea but one of the earliest recorded flights of a sailor's imagination.

It is not surprising that the tale comes from an Egyptian merchant sailing the Red Sea. Although the first men to venture from shore in floating craft—dugouts or reed rafts, perhaps—may have done so almost anywhere, the first documented seafarers were Egyptians and Mesopotamians. Carved on rocks in southern Egypt are hundreds of crude sketches of ships dating back to about 3000 B.C.; some of the vessels portrayed are even rigged with simple sails. Egyptian pottery of the same period is decorated with similar ships. And at the site of Eridu in Mesopotamia, excavators have found a clay model of a boat made as early as 3500 B.C. It resembles a skiff; but on the interior planking forward of amidships is a socket that could have supported a mast, and on both gunwales are holes that could have secured stays. If the boat did indeed have a mast, this is the most ancient sailing craft known, more than 5,000 years old.

The mariners of Egypt and Mesopotamia, nosing out of the Nile, Tigris and Euphrates Rivers, rarely went far beyond sight of land. After them would come a succession of farther-ranging seafarers. The hardy and daring Minoans would extend the sea routes of the civilized world northward and westward from the island of Crete in the Second Millennium B.C. Maritime supremacy would then pass to the Phoenicians and the Greeks, both of whom spread trading outposts across the Mediterranean, and finally to a nation of former landlubbers: the Romans. Under the Romans, the great sea would be commanded by a single power for the only time in history. Its huge basin—a vast marine highway for administrators, merchandise, ideas—was the heart of their world, and they would hold sway there until seafaring declined into the Dark Ages in the Fifth Century A.D.

These, then, were the ancient mariners. The first humble traders to venture into the Mediterranean and the Persian Gulf three millennia earlier could not, of course, have had the faintest premonition of what they were setting in motion. Yet the lure of the watery distances quickly proved irresistible even to them. By 2650 B.C. the eastern Mediterranean carried a busy traffic of cargo ships between Egypt and the ports of Byblos, Tyre and Sidon on the coasts of Syria and Palestine. That year a Pharaoh's scribe recorded the "bringing of 40 ships filled with cedar logs." The durable, fragrant wood of the cedar became a favorite commodity of the Egyptians; it provided coffins for the mummies of their rulers, oil for their embalming—and timbers and planking for more vessels to bring in more cedar logs.

The ships that made these early voyages were long, lean and graceful. Like gondolas, they curved from tall, upswept bows to high fanlike sterns. They were built by an ingenious method that would remain in favor among the Egyptians for many centuries. The Greek historian Herodotus, visiting Egypt in about 450 B.C., likened it to bricklaying. The shipyard workers fastened short sections of hull planking together, usually with rope made of braided grass, and then added supporting ribs and timbers. Since the wood they employed was relatively light, they strengthened the hull with a truss—a heavy rope, strung from bow to stern. A bar in the center of the rope was twisted like a tourniquet to brace the ends of the hull and help the ship withstand the strain of a heavy sea.

The earliest Egyptian masts were unlike any used before or since: They were double. Because the vessels were without keels and had only a few light ribs, their hulls could not support the thrust of a single mast. So the Egyptians fashioned a two-legged version that distributed the pressure on the hull; the legs were joined at the top. The double mast was secured in place by forestays and backstays, and it carried a square expanse of linen that was stretched between a yard at the top and a boom at the foot. The rig had one significant drawback: Trimming of the sail was impeded by the spread-legged mast; hence the wind had to be off the quarter or astern.

But the cargo vessel also carried oarsmen, and when the wind blew from the wrong direction or died, the crew simply unstepped the mast and stowed it. Out came the oars, which were fitted through rope oarlocks, and the men bent to their work—or, more accurately, rose and fell at their work: The early Egyptian oarsman stood up from his bench, then sat slowly down as he pulled the blade through the water. Because of his method of rowing, the most important piece of clothing for an

Egyptian oarsman was a patch of leather on the rear of his loincloth, to serve as a cushion and to protect his buttocks from chafing. Steering was also performed with oars—three on either side of the stern, wielded by the helmsmen.

By the middle of the Second Millennium B.C., the Egyptians began building vessels with stronger internal bracing, although their ships still had no keel and used a bow-to-stern truss to provide the necessary support. They had replaced the double mast with a single one that allowed the sail to swing in a wider arc. They also designed wider sails and, for ease of handling, sometimes abandoned the boom along the foot, replacing it with brails—lines that were run from the yard, looped under the foot of the sail, and used to furl the linen expanse. Some of these craft were remarkably sturdy and efficient, capable of carrying huge granite obelisks weighing hundreds of tons 120 miles along the Nile from the quarries of Aswan to the great temple cities of Karnak and Luxor.

During the first half of the Second Millennium foreign invasions had caused seaborne commerce to languish. But the Red Sea trade was revived around 1500 B.C. by the first great woman ruler in history, Queen Hatshepsut, who sent whole fleets of ships south into the Red Sea in search of cargoes. They carried Egyptian goods for barter—daggers, hatchets and necklaces. In return they got incense, ivory, gold, hides and ebony. Some of the Egyptian traders loaded myrrh trees, their roots bagged for planting at home; the trees yielded an aromatic resin that was burned in Egyptian temples. Others carried home cattle, dogs, monkeys, apes and once, wrote a scribe, "a southern panther alive, captured for Her Majesty." Still others took aboard inhabitants of the lands around the Red Sea—whether free or as slaves the scribes do not say.

For another three centuries or so, despite periodic harassment by pirates and amphibious invaders, wealthy Egyptians continued to enjoy the benefits of a sophisticated maritime commerce. They imported cattle

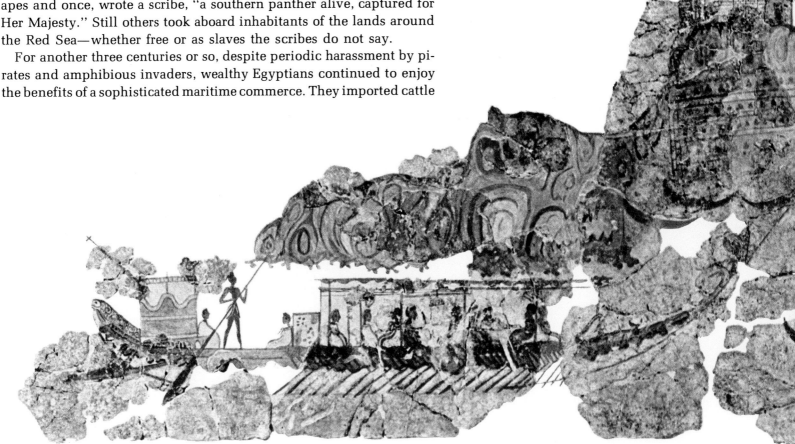

from Asia Minor, built homes of rare Syrian lumber, decorated them with African ivory and filled them with the smell of Arabian incense. They ate delicacies from the orchards of Cyprus on plates of Cypriote copper. They dressed in cloth from Syria and jewelry made of silver from Asia Minor. Some of these imports they transshipped, along with Egypt's own papyrus writing paper, linen, beads, figurines and jars of oil. The commercial lifeblood of Egypt throbbed through the expanding ports; the great riverine metropolis of Memphis attracted so many overseas traders that the city had a special foreign quarter. Memphis had no wharves; the vessels simply pulled up on the beach to load and unload their cargoes. Merchants and sailors thronged the shore, and customs officials bustled about, making sure that the Pharaoh's tariffs were paid.

Even in their trading heyday, the Egyptians did not venture beyond the Red Sea and the southeastern corner of the Mediterranean. Exploration beyond the horizon remained for less powerful nations with more daring seamen, among them the remarkable Minoan civilization on the island of Crete.

A detail from a fresco found on the island of Thera in the Aegean Sea provides a rare glimpse of a Minoan ship—this one a canopied, paddle-driven vessel whose robed passengers may be engaged in a religious procession.

The Minoans were a dark, elegant people of mysterious origin. Even their ancient name is unknown; they were given the name of Minoans by a modern-day British archeologist, Arthur Evans, who derived it from Greek mythology: Minos was a legendary King of Crete who ordered the building of a labyrinth to house a preternatural creature with the body of a man and the head of a bull. The beast, known as the Minotaur, lived on human sacrifices. Evans first encountered the people he called Minoans in 1900, when he discovered the ruins of a sprawling, mazelike palace on the north coast of Crete. Images of a bull were scattered through the rooms, along with countless fragments of graceful pottery and clay tablets covered with a writing that has never been deciphered.

The spread of Minoan exploration and culture can be traced through the evidence of similar artifacts. As early as 2000 B.C. the Egyptian Pharaoh Amenemhet II included Minoan silver bowls among the treasures in his tomb. Between 1800 and 1500 B.C. Minoan vessels sailed to ports throughout the eastern Mediterranean and as far as Sicily in the west, opening up trade routes that would be used for centuries thereafter. And the Minoans created such a powerful navy that—alone among ancient civilizations—they built their cities without walls.

Perhaps that was a mistake. On the peninsula and islands directly to the north lived aggressive tribesmen who had come down through Macedonia. These people, known as the Achaeans, were the first Greeks. Soon they were trading with the Minoans—and imitating them as well. Achaeans wore Minoan jewelry and designed their own in the same style; Achaean soldiers carried Minoan-style swords; and Achaean women favored Minoan hairstyles and dresses, tight at the waist with an open bodice. Inevitably, they coveted the Minoans' island as well. The archeological evidence indicates that they overran the island in about 1450 B.C. Crete now became part of a vast trading empire that was culturally Greek.

For another 200 years and more, the Achaeans sailed far and wide in the Mediterranean; they established colonies in Sicily, on the island of Rhodes and along the coast of Syria. There is even evidence of an Achaean colony in Egypt itself—the onetime mercantile giant that the hard-sailing traders from the north had almost eclipsed.

Of Achaean ships, little is known. A few models, vase paintings and engravings on seals give only a tantalizing glimpse of the vessels that were responsible for the first great commercial empire: deep, rounded hulls and spider webs of lines indicating a large spread of sail. The riches the ships brought to Crete are better documented. Achaean merchant princes rode about the hilly island in chariots, lived in immense mansions, wore richly woven clothes and drank from golden goblets. Even in warfare they displayed a taste for splendor: Their officers fought in elaborately engraved armor.

But at sea their martial prowess proved to have limits. All through the recent centuries of trade and exploration in the Mediterranean, merchantmen and seacoast dwellers alike had been victims of intermittent piracy. Solitary corsairs chased down cargo vessels, bands of waterborne brigands attacked trading fleets, and other small flotillas descended on ports and looted them. The Achaean navy, though evidently strong

A royal relic of shipbuilding

The best-preserved vessel of antiquity is also the oldest. Buried in a pit at the foot of the Great Pyramid at Giza, a royal barge of the Egyptian Pharaoh Cheops lay untouched for 4,500 years, until it was discovered accidentally in 1954 amid the rubble of previous explorations. Evidently it had taken its owner down the Nile to his tomb and had been left there to ferry him to the afterworld.

The tomb, protected by blocks of limestone and sealed with gypsum plaster, was virtually airtight and watertight, and most of the barge's wood was intact. Unaccountably, the Pharaoh's subjects had disassembled the vessel into 1,224 separate pieces, which were stacked in 13 distinct layers in the pit. Archeologists therefore learned the details of ancient Egyptian shipbuilding the hard way, by having to rebuild the royal ship from its component parts. The project took more than 10 years.

The rebuilders discovered that the Egyptians of the Third Millennium B.C. constructed their ships as the Greeks and Romans did after them: from the outside in, first fastening the planks of the hull together, then strengthening the structure with interior ribs. The modern method of ship construction—laying the keel, then raising the ribs and finally fastening the hull planking over them—was not developed until the Middle Ages.

Buried with the wooden sections of the royal craft were thousands of yards of alfa-grass rope, which the archeologists at first took to be rigging. Only after much trial-and-error reconstruction did they realize that Cheops' vessel was actually tied together (page 14) so that the contraction of the wet rope and expansion of the wet wood tightened the fit of the planks and helped seal the seams.

Today Cheops' reconstructed barge has its own museum, near the Great Pyramid at Giza. But it sits in lonely isolation, virtually as secluded as it had been when it was in the tomb—and in worse condition. Having survived interment for thousands of years with little ill effect, the royal vessel, once it was above ground, began deteriorating under the onslaught of humidity and temperature variations.

The top layer of the dismantled barge and the tip of one oar, shown as they were found in their tomb, are juxtaposed with an ivory statuette of Cheops—the only portrait of him known to exist.

With its oars lashed erect, Cheops' reconstructed barge presents a picture of royal comfort. The Pharaoh's stateroom is aft (right) and his courtiers' area forward. The canopy at the bow may have been used to shelter an idol or a high priest.

Early Egyptian shipbuilders made Cheops' barge watertight by weaving grass ropes through seam holes (1, at right) in the hull planking; when wet, the ropes shrank, the planks and battens (2) swelled, and the seams closed. Ribs (3) were laid on top of the planks, and stanchions (4) were fastened to the ribs to support a beam (5). The beam, in turn, held perpendicular deck beams (6).

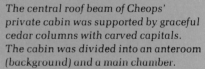

The barge's oars were held by flexible lashings that served as oarlocks. The simpler lashing at left holds an oar at rest.

The central roof beam of Cheops' private cabin was supported by graceful cedar columns with carved capitals. The cabin was divided into an anteroom (background) and a main chamber.

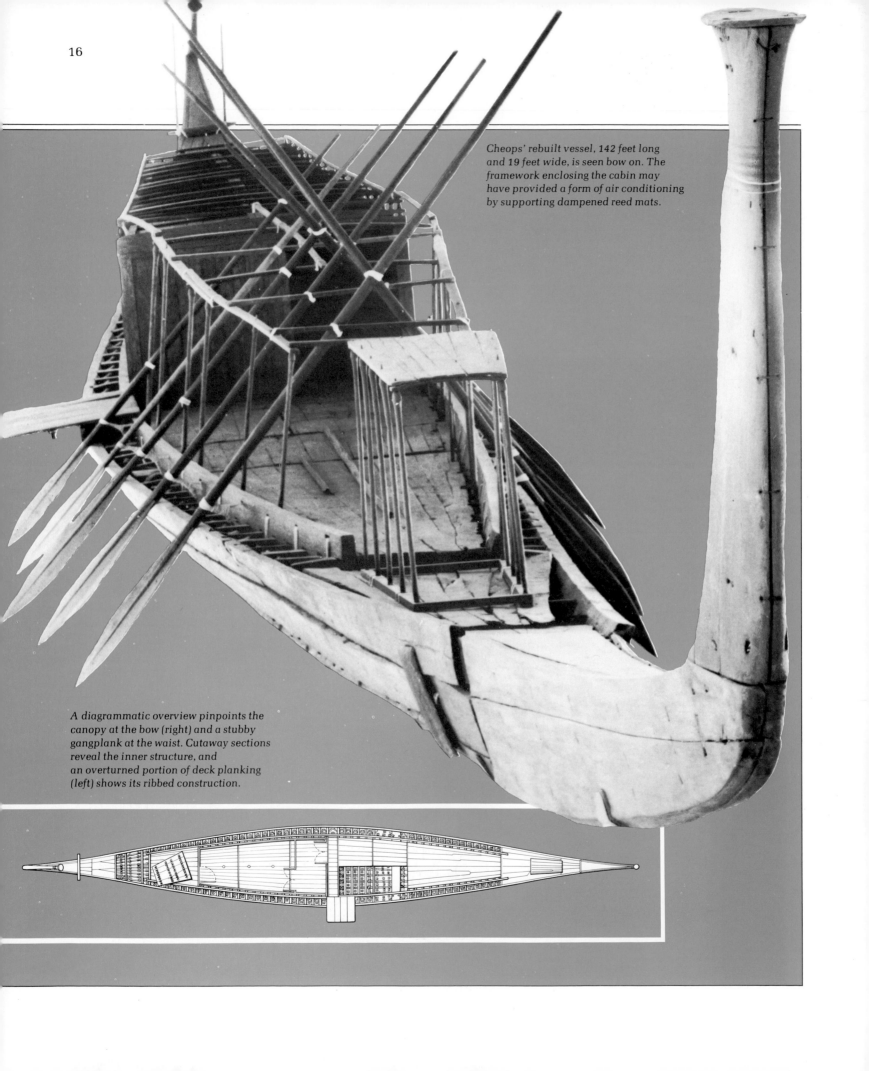

Cheops' rebuilt vessel, 142 feet long and 19 feet wide, is seen bow on. The framework enclosing the cabin may have provided a form of air conditioning by supporting dampened reed mats.

A diagrammatic overview pinpoints the canopy at the bow (right) and a stubby gangplank at the waist. Cutaway sections reveal the inner structure, and an overturned portion of deck planking (left) shows its ribbed construction.

enough to defeat the Minoans, did not sufficiently police the seas against these pirates. Their harassment increased, and by about 1200 B.C. the era of maritime traders was giving way to a dark age of maritime invaders. These outlaws were known simply as the "Sea Peoples."

The most dramatic account of their depredations comes from a scribe of the Egyptian Pharaoh Ramses III, writing in 1190 B.C.: "Lo, the northern countries, which are in their isles, are restless in their limbs; they infest the ways of the harbor mouths." He was describing a massive and chaotic invasion—as much a migration as a military campaign. Thousands of seafarers from many coastal towns had joined together to move south along the Palestinian shore, ravaging as they went. Part of their force traveled on land—women, children and supplies rumbling along in two-wheeled oxcarts, and the men marching ahead. But a more formidable contingent came by sea. As they swept south their numbers swelled, many of their intended victims siding with them when they could not beat them off. Apparently some of the raiders were Achaeans, opportunistic members of the same tribal group that had conquered the Minoans almost 300 years earlier.

Amid the invading force was a band of menacing warriors who wore only feathered headdresses and loincloths as they poured ashore wielding swords and heavy-headed spears. Their near-nakedness and their waving headgear lent them a savage glamor, instilling dread in all who confronted them. "No land could stand before their arms," wrote Ramses' scribe, and then, referring to the devastation by the land force: "They came with fire prepared before them forward to Egypt."

What followed was the first major naval battle of which a contemporary description has survived: Ramses had the scene depicted afterward on the wall of a temple near Thebes. Evidently overconfident, the raiders descended on a port in the Nile delta without bothering to stow their sails and row into battle in the customary manner. The Egyptians let them file through the harbor mouth unopposed, then pounced.

Out from the shores of the harbor poured a squadron of Egyptian war galleys. The invaders turned to meet them, swords and spears at the ready. They planned to board Ramses' galleys and cut the defenders to bits, but the Egyptians had conceived a different strategy, based on their knowledge of a fatal flaw in the attackers' arsenal. The invaders, unlike Ramses' forces, lacked bows and arrows.

So while the Sea Peoples prepared for a crunch of galleys and a melee on deck, the Egyptians slowed, then stopped. They had encircled the enemy vessels, and they came to a halt just within arrow range. Suddenly the air was filled with a hissing downpour of bronze-tipped shafts. The unarmored raiders were helpless against the arrows, and soon the decks of the invading flotilla were littered with bodies. To the deadly tempest from the Egyptian galleys was added a storm of missiles and larger arrows loosed by soldiers lining the shores nearby. The raiders scrambled to get out their oars and close with the defenders, but the low bulwarks of their vessels gave no protection to the oarsmen; they were riddled by arrows where they sat. One by one the invading galleys drifted out of position, the rowers slumped over their benches. And now the defenders moved in.

Dropping their bows, they took up spears and battle maces as their oarsmen pulled them alongside the demoralized enemy. The shields of the foe were no match for the Egyptians' swinging maces, and the northerners were now heavily outnumbered. Galley after galley was swept clear. Many of the invaders' light, slender warships were capsized and their occupants hurled into the water. Most drowned; those who managed to swim toward shore were met with a barrage of arrows as they staggered onto the beach.

Ramses' victory was complete. But it did not bring an end to the era of marauding, although Egypt itself would never again be the target of a large-scale attack from the sea. Those few invaders who managed to slip out of the Egyptian net split up and fled back northward and eastward to attack and occupy Palestine. Others headquartered themselves in fortress towns among the islands and shores of Greece, and they spread fear through half the Mediterranean for 200 years.

The operations of the Sea Peoples were swift and savage. First, a group of raiders would gather to plot an attack on a prosperous port. Often the town would be reconnoitered surreptitiously at night. At dawn their galleys would pour into the harbor; the raiders would rush ashore, fanning out through the town, pillaging and burning as they went. Success depended on surprise and speed. Within an hour or so the galleys would be crammed with loot—gold and silver dishes, jewels, valuable ornaments. Even cattle could be herded aboard galleys brought along for the purpose. But the raiders' prize booty was human: women who could be sold as concubines, and boys and girls as servants. A bustling slave trade developed in some seacoast towns, stimulated by these forays. And in the same markets the pirates could barter their plunder of valuables.

A vivid glimpse of this era survives in a papyrus journal written by an Egyptian priest named Wenamon, who presided over a temple dedicated to Amon, the supreme deity of Egypt. As a high official of the Egyptian clergy, Wenamon was assigned the sacred task of procuring wood to build a ceremonial barge that would carry an image of Amon along the Nile in an annual observance. Syria's cedars were considered the finest wood available, and Wenamon was ordered by the high priest of Egypt to voyage there to arrange the purchase. Carrying a bag filled with seven and a half pounds of silver for his transactions and armed with a small image of Amon to bless his travels, he set sail for the Syrian port of Byblos on a spring day in about 1100 B.C. (his journal gives the date, April 20, but not the year).

A swift pirate ship (right), fitted with a ram that would be used if a patrolling naval vessel took the raiders by surprise, swoops down on a Greek merchantman in a Sixth Century B.C. vase painting. This encounter would have ended with the pirates grappling alongside their victim, then boarding and looting her.

His ship's first port of call was a town named Dor, near present-day Haifa on the coast of Palestine. Dor, it happened, was one of the ports that had been occupied by sea raiders; they were called Tjekers, and some of their ancestors had taken part in the disastrous attack on the Nile delta. Although the occupiers continued to engage in occasional raids, they allowed maritime commerce to go on as usual in Dor, supplementing their ill-got gains with legitimate taxes and customs duties. Arriving there, Wenamon's vessel was not disturbed; in fact the local chieftain, Beder, greeted him with gifts of beef, bread and wine. On the morning after his arrival, however, Wenamon discovered that the attractions of a life of piracy had been too tempting for one of the ship's company, who had deserted, taking along the priest's bag of silver. Counting on his religious status to give him impunity, Wenamon accused Beder of collusion and demanded that his silver be returned. When Beder protested innocence, Wenamon badgered him to hunt down the culprit. His manner was so insistent that he soon found himself forcibly encouraged to resume his journey toward Byblos.

En route he did a curious thing, which may be accounted for by a combination of frustration, priestly arrogance and the standards of morality during this era. In another port, evidently Sidon, Wenamon encountered some Tjekers and turned the tables by robbing them—the journal does not say how. "I am taking your money," he explained, "and keeping it until you find mine. Was it not a man of Tjeker who stole it?" The logic of Wenamon's reasoning may have escaped his victims. In any case, events were to demonstrate the unwisdom of taking revenge on men who lived by marauding.

Wenamon had scarcely sailed into the harbor at Byblos when he was told by the harbor master to sail out again. Word of his transgression had preceded him; evidently the ruling prince of Byblos, Zakar-Baal, feared reprisal if the culprit were sheltered. But Wenamon ignored the order.

Every day thereafter, Byblos' harbor master told Wenamon to leave. Every day Wenamon refused. And every day Zakar-Baal did nothing to enforce his harbor master's order. Clearly, the prince was worried that Tjekers might come sailing into his harbor at any moment. He wanted to be able to report that he had repeatedly instructed their enemy to leave. At the same time, he was reluctant to lose an affluent customer; in fact, he was so desirous of keeping Wenamon content that, at one point, he supplied the priest with some meat, wine and the companionship of a dancing girl (far from turning the latter gift down, the priest even recorded her name in his journal—Tanetnot).

This charade went on for a month. After interminable haggling, a deal was made and the cedar wood Wenamon had been ordered to purchase was delivered to the beach for loading. Just then, 11 ships manned by Tjekers sailed into the harbor. They immediately demanded that Zakar-Baal arrest the priest. Wenamon reports in his journal that he sat on the beach and cried.

Zakar-Baal now demonstrated new depths of cunning. "I cannot arrest a messenger of Amon in my territory," he explained to the raiders; "let me send him off and then you chase him."

Wenamon had no choice. Zakar-Baal supplied him with a ship under charter, loaded the lumber, collected his money and sent Wenamon out into the arms of the pirates. But at this point the god Amon must at last have come to Wenamon's rescue. Scarcely was he in the open sea, running for his life with the Tjekers in hot pursuit, when a southeasterly gale swept up the coast. Driven before it, Wenamon's ship ran northward to a place of refuge he called Alasia (probably Cyprus). The Tjekers, fearing that their light galleys would be swamped in the stormy seas, made for the nearest shore, letting their quarry escape.

Wenamon's troubles were not yet over. He was threatened with death by the inhabitants of Alasia, who had doubtlessly suffered from pirates and thought Wenamon was one. Luck was with him again. He was saved by the intercession of the local Queen. The rest of his journal is lost, but there is little doubt that he managed to reach home again: His narrative was found buried in Egyptian sands 3,000 years later.

The simple tale of Wenamon stands in intriguing contrast to the far more renowned accounts of sea raiders composed by the Greek poet Homer. His epics were created around 800 B.C. or even later—some 400 years after the Sea Peoples had disappeared from history. But Homer knew of them—or more specifically, of the Achaeans—from a great oral tradition carried on by generations of bards.

Although he cast the Achaeans in a heroic mold, Homer's epics have the ring of truth. For example, Odysseus, the hero of the *Odyssey,* wishing to conceal his identity at one point during his adventures, misleads a shepherd with a story that he obviously expects to be believed because it is so typical of the time. He is, he claims, a sea raider from Crete. With his little fleet of nine vessels, he had sailed to Egypt, "and there in the Nile I brought my curved ships to. And now I ordered my good men to stay by the ships on guard while I sent out some scouts to reconnoiter from the heights. But these ran amuck and in a trice, carried away by their own violence, they had plundered some of the fine Egyptian farms, borne off the women and children and killed the men. The hue and cry soon

A Sixth Century vase painting portrays the crew of a Greek warship. Pairs of oarsmen, protected by shields, row to the beat of a drummer amidships, while a lookout mans the bow (left) and a helmsman handles the steering oar at the stern. The bottom panel dramatizes what may have been marine combat.

reached the city, and the townsfolk, roused by the alarm, turned out at dawn. The whole place was filled with infantry and chariots and the glint of arms." The expedition, says Odysseus, ended in disaster: Most of his men were cut down or captured and enslaved.

Such forays were, of course, the stock in trade of the Sea Peoples—and generally ended more successfully. By glorifying them (Odysseus proudly called himself "sacker of cities") Homer was celebrating the boldness of what he regarded as an Achaean aristocracy.

Nor was the *Odyssey* his only celebration of Achaean glamor. One of history's most famous amphibious expeditions—famous solely because of Homer—occurred about the same time that Ramses III was beating off the invading Sea Peoples. Around 1200 B.C. a loose confederacy of Achaean war lords under Agamemnon, King of Mycenae in Peloponnesian Greece, united against the rich city of Troy, located across the Aegean in Asia Minor. In the *Iliad*, Homer's narrative of the war on Troy, the Achaeans' exploits take on a legendary glow. The very names of their chiefs—Agamemnon, Achilles, Ajax, Odysseus—have become household words; and so entangled are reality and myth that only the broad outlines of the expedition are discernible.

For whatever cause—the abduction of a Greek chief's beautiful wife by a Trojan prince, or mere piratical greed—a powerful Achaean fleet assembled in a lonely cove of eastern Greece and set sail in the teeth of summer winds. Homer describes the ships in loving detail. Twenty-oared and 50-oared galleys, with a few heavy troop transports propelled by as many as 100 rowers, they were the most formidable warships of their day. Built on frames of ribs and keels, their jointed planks—oak, poplar, or pine—formed long, gently rounded hulls, which were smeared with a sealant of pitch. Their painted bows and sterns reared abruptly from the water line, after the fashion of the old Minoan ships, and ended in a graceful curve, so that Homer compared them to the "straight horns" of cattle.

Inside, except for small decks fore and aft, long lines of rowers' benches filled the hull, with the oars bound to tholepins by leather thongs. The single mast amidships could be raised and lowered, and it carried a linen square sail, with rigging of twisted papyrus fiber. Wide-bladed steering oars, one on each quarter, guided the vessel. The largest of the Achaean war galleys probably measured some 90 feet in length and about 20 feet in width amidships.

These vessels could not stay at sea very long. Usually they were drawn up on the beach at nighttime. So a city like Troy could not be blockaded in the ordinary sense, by ships on constant patrol. Instead Homer's heroes landed on the nearby shore and laid siege to the city walls. Homer's claim that the war lasted 10 years must be an exaggeration. But certainly the city did fall—whether through the ruse of the Trojan horse or by some other means is unknown.

The return home of the Greek raiders was as perilous as the siege had been. During a violent storm, many of their ships were dashed to bits on the rocky shores of the Peloponnesus. Odysseus was driven far out to sea by another storm and, largely because of the enmity of Poseidon, god of the sea, was destined to roam the Mediterranean for years (pages 32-39).

Even more than the *Iliad*, the *Odyssey* is an inextricable blend of fact and fiction. It overflows with fabulous monsters and perils, yet the tale is also rich in information about ancient seafaring. Homer points out, for example, that Achaean mariners navigated by certain constellations in the night sky: the Pleiades, Boötes, and Arktos—"the only one," Homer notes, "which never bathes in Ocean's Stream" (i.e., does not set beneath the horizon).

His description of Odysseus' ships is equally explicit. They were light, 20-oared galleys. Of the warriors aboard, all were used to pulling the oar except the captain-helmsman, the bow lookout, and the time beater, who paced the rowers. The men rowed not only in battle and when entering or leaving harbor, but also when becalmed, or simply to take advantage of a favorable wind. The oars, says Homer, were "the wings of the ship." But at times the galleys were propelled only by the wind; then the men attended to the rigging, or sat at ease on their benches while the captain-helmsman kept watch from the small deck astern.

In telling of a storm at sea, Homer provides the clearest clues to the rigging of Odysseus' vessel—a single mast held in place by a backstay and two forestays fastened to each side of the bow. One day, Odysseus says, a "howling wind suddenly sprang up from the west and hit us with hurricane force. The squall snapped both forestays together. As the mast fell aft, all the rigging tumbled into the bilge, and the mast itself, reaching the stern, struck the helmsman on the head and smashed in all the bones of his skull."

Homer even describes how a galley was constructed—a task that was forced on Odysseus (and completed with the assistance of the goddess Calypso) after a shipwreck. The passage is the first account of shipbuilding in literature, and would have served any marine architect of the ancient world. After cutting down 20 trees and lopping off their branches, Odysseus "smoothed them carefully, and adzed them straight and square. Then he bored them and made them fast to one another with dowels and battens. He laid out the bottom as wide as a good shipwright would for a beamy freighter. He set up close-set ribs, made half decks fast to them, and finished up by adding the long side-planking. He stepped a mast and yard and added a broad oar to steer with. He fenced the hull about with a latticed bulwark to keep the water out, and he heaped brush upon it. The goddess brought him cloth for a sail; he fashioned a fine one. He rigged braces, brails and sheets and, putting the craft on rollers, hauled it down to the sea."

The ship did not last: The gods (and Homer) could not resist another wreck—complete with that nightmare of all sailors, a storm beating against a rock-walled lee shore. The handsome mariner was rescued by a

As imagined by a Roman sculptor, Homer's Achaean hero Odysseus betrays the price of 10 years of sea wanderings in his worn and watchful expression. The statue evidently depicts him in the beggar's disguise that he assumed on his return home to Greece after voyaging throughout the Mediterranean.

Odysseus' helmsman, knocked flat by the sea monster Scylla, hangs on to save himself from falling overboard in this Roman sculpture. When the sculpture was discovered in Sperlonga, Italy, the top of the helmsman's head and the tip of the port steering oar were missing.

beautiful damsel, who took him to her father, the King of the island of Phaeacia, where Odysseus had washed ashore. The King entertained him, provided another ship for him and sent him on his way. Finally, after 10 years filled with adventure enough for any mariner, Odysseus returned to his family and his island kingdom.

Odysseus, driven by the gods and the winds, was an involuntary explorer. But during the same era, the 12th Century B.C., history's first recorded journey of intentional exploration was led by another Achaean hero nearly as well remembered: Jason. The expedition of Jason and his Argonauts (sailors of the ship *Argo*—"the swift") was a saga so well-loved that ancient poets were still embellishing it a thousand years after the journey was thought to have taken place. The many different versions flagrantly contradicted one another; they became barnacled with romantic incidents and a fabulous bestiary, and later writers recruited numberless heroes to the ship's crew, including Hercules and Orpheus.

At the heart of the story, though, there seems to lie the record of an actual journey of discovery that opened up the Black Sea to eventual

Deities and demons of the deep

The uncharted Mediterranean fascinated and frightened the ancient Greeks, who attempted to explain its mysteries by peopling the watery world with all manner of deities and demons. Storms, for example, were blamed on the violent whims of a sea-god named Poseidon. Other disasters were attributed to malevolent monsters that often took the form of undulating serpents. On the other hand, benign supernatural beings called Nereids kept watch over sailors and helped extricate them from peril.

The mythic denizens of the deep were believed to be in frequent conflict with one another or with mortals—accounting for the sudden changes in fortune that mariners sometimes experienced. A favorite figure in the imagined struggle was the Greek demigod Herakles (later the Romans' Hercules). His heroic confrontations with evil adversaries, ranging from the many-headed Hydra *(below)* to a horned serpent, provided a frequent motif in the paintings and bas-reliefs that adorned Greek pottery—the source of most of the images here.

The Hydra, a nine-headed water serpent, struggles with Herakles (below), who attacks it with his sword. For each head he cut off, two grew in its place.

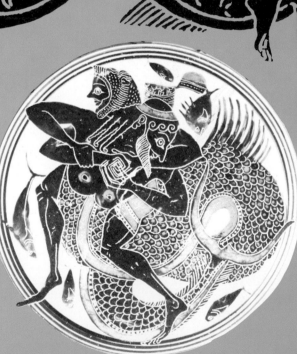

As curious dolphins watch (above), the long-haired sea monster Triton—half man and half fish—provides Herakles with another opportunity to test his strength.

With a trident under his arm, the sea-god Poseidon (left) rides a hippocampus, a monster that has the forequarters of a horse and the tail of a fish.

Achelous (right), an enormous horned water serpent, meets its match as Herakles breaks off one of its horns. From Achelous' blood, the beguiling sirens of Homer's Odyssey supposedly sprang.

A Nereid takes a wild ride on a hippocampus in this bas-relief on a cover for a box or vase. Nereids were sailors' favorite deities because they supposedly protected them from shipwreck.

Greek trade and colonization. Shorn of much (but not all) fantasy, the account goes something like this. In the land of the Minyae, a shadowy people who occupied part of Thessaly and of Boeotia in central Greece, the legitimate King was overthrown by his brother, Pelias. Prince Jason, son of the dethroned King, was dispatched on a dangerous voyage of exploration by Pelias, who hoped to destroy him. Jason's mission, it seems, was a quest for wealth or trade, symbolized by the mysterious Golden Fleece, a legendary and priceless treasure that lay far to the east, over uncharted seas.

The Argonauts' passage across the Aegean exposed them to storms at sea, monsters and seductive women. Less seductive were a group of winged females who accosted Jason and his men in the narrow Bosporus strait: These were the Harpies, a particularly repulsive swarm of pests who, like sea gulls fouling the ship, disgusted the sailors by defecating on their food. No sooner had the Argonauts beaten off these creatures than the *Argo* came to an obstacle far more dreadful. At the end of the strait, near the mouth of the Black Sea, stood the terrible Symplegades, the "Clashing Rocks," which rushed together and smashed anything that tried to pass between them.

To test the speed of these rocks, the Argonauts contrived a ruse: They sent a dove flying through the strait. As they watched, the awesome cliffs surged together so fast that they clipped the bird's tail feathers. But there was no other way past the strait, so the Argonauts advanced cautiously and prepared to rush through as quickly as possible. They soon had no choice: A "backwash, overtaking them," wrote the Greek poet Apollonius in the most finished version of the epic, "thrust the *Argo* in between the rocks. Then the fears of all were turned to panic." A towering wave came toward them through the passage. Only the adroitness of the steersman saved the *Argo* from capsizing. He took the great billow head on. The *Argo's* bow rose up over the wave, which slid harmlessly under her keel.

With everyone pulling and the oars bending under the strain, the *Argo* could make no headway against the current rushing between the cliffs. Another comber came toward them; the *Argo* rose over it. Then, as she lay in the trough between waves, the great rocks closed in. They clashed together like a stone vise. Miraculously they caught only the ship's figurehead, shearing it off. And as they parted to clash together again, the *Argo* was caught by another current that swept her through, into the open sea on the other side.

The description of the Symplegades, seemingly wild fantasy, may well have stemmed from ancient sailors' actual encounters with icebergs, or a single enormous iceberg. These massive blue floes (the Symplegades were also called the "Blue" or the "Wandering Rocks") frequently drifted down the Russian rivers into the Black Sea. And as mariners since the Argonauts have discovered, a big iceberg, melting from the top, can resemble two ice cliffs, though retaining the same huge underwater base. Such a berg, especially when stranded in a narrow strait, can groan and grind, swirl and roll, and its disintegrating cliffs may suddenly smash down onto anything floating through the gap of water at the surface. In the case of a galley such as the *Argo*, the toppling

In this Roman relief, Jason's ship Argo is readied for her epic voyage in search of the Golden Fleece. Assisted by the goddess Athena (left), the Argo's pilot adjusts a yard while a shipwright works with mallet and chisel to finish off the stern.

ice towers could have created just the current needed to wash the ship through to safety.

The Argonauts now found themselves rowing along the southern shores of the Black Sea. The Greeks eventually named it the Euxine or "friendly" sea; but to these explorers it was unknown and, thus far, threatening. Nevertheless they pushed on; and at the eastern limit, where the ranges of the Caucasus lifted steeply into the sky, they found the land of Aia, or Colchis. Here lived King Aeëtes, owner of the legendary Fleece. He greeted the Argonauts with hostility.

The Golden Fleece lends itself to many explanations. Some have thought that it was the symbol of a scroll containing the secret of alchemy; others that it was an emblem of sunlight. But the Roman geographer Strabo offered perhaps the most plausible explanation, when he wrote of the Black Sea that "still in this region fleeces are fastened to the bottom of streams where there are shallows, and gold-bearing rocks drop gold in the wool. Then, thus loaded, these fleeces are carried to the furnace and burned, and the gold is easily collected.'' This was an early kind of alluvial gold panning—or, more accurately, netting. Thus, gold itself could have been the true quest of the *Argo*.

King Aeëtes, by most accounts, first resisted the Argonauts by guile, setting Jason a list of superhuman tasks to perform before he could have the Golden Fleece. Then Aeëtes' guile gave way to threat and refusal. But in the meantime, a woman came to the rescue: King Aeëtes' daughter Medea fell in love with Jason. With her help, and in her company, the Argonauts made off with the Golden Fleece.

Despite their escape, the story ended tragically. Jason and Medea conspired in the murder of King Pelias, who still ruled Jason's homeland of Minyae. But Pelias' son Acastus drove the pair into exile. Their marriage ended in mutual distrust, in the murder of their children—evidently by Medea's own hand—and in Medea's lonely wanderings among the petty kingdoms of Greece. As for Jason, who had forfeited the favor of the gods by abandoning Medea, he roamed wretchedly about the world for years, finally returning as an old man to his homeland. There, while he rested nostalgically under the rotting frame of the *Argo*, the ship's bow broke loose, toppled onto him and killed him.

Because of the spellbinding epics of Homer and other Greek poets, the Achaeans are the best-known seafarers of this era. By contrast, the Phoenicians, a contemporary maritime people, are wrapped in mystery—yet their greatness is unarguable.

About 3000 B.C. the Phoenicians had established their homeland along the narrow coast at the foot of the Syrian mountains. Pressed against the shores, they naturally looked seaward. As early as the Third Millennium they had begun living primarily by seagoing commerce, and by the Ninth Century B.C., after the menace of the Sea Peoples receded, they were sending their deep-hulled, high-railed vessels far to the west and spreading colonies all around the Mediterranean. The very names of the cities they founded—Tyre, Sidon and, most important of all, Carthage (near the site of present-day Tunis on the north coast of Africa)—are redolent of ships.

The lure of trade led the Phoenicians to Sardinia, Sicily—even out into the Atlantic and along the land of Tartessus, as the Spanish coast was then called. There they found tin, which could be fused with copper—widely available in the Mediterranean—to produce bronze. By about 800 B.C. the Phoenicians had established their westernmost outpost at the site now known as Cádiz.

Sometime around 600 B.C. the Phoenicians seem to have accomplished an unprecedented exploit: According to the Greek historian Herodotus, they circumnavigated the continent of Africa. The voyage was in a clockwise direction. "They sailed from the Red Sea into the Indian Ocean," wrote Herodotus, "and each autumn they put in at some favorable place on the African coast." There they set up camp for the winter, sowed seed "and awaited the harvest next year." In the spring, with their holds full of grain, "they put to sea again, and two years later reached the Pillars of Hercules," as the headlands flanking the Strait of

In a Greek vase painting, the legendary Achaean hero Jason is rescued from the jaws of a serpent by his divine protector Athena. Suspended on a bough that hangs above him is the object of his expedition—the Golden Fleece.

Gibraltar were called. By the end of the third year they had crossed the Mediterranean and were home.

For all their extraordinary accomplishments, the Phoenicians were a secretive people. Although they invented the Western alphabet, they left almost no record of themselves. They guarded their trade by surrounding it with nightmarish rumors of sea monsters and shipwrecks, or by keeping canny silence.

In gaining a position of eminence in Mediterranean commerce, they were inadvertently aided by waves of Greek tribesmen who had continued to pour down from the north and had gradually overrun the Achaeans. As the Achaean civilization crumbled into ruin, the Phoenicians even established a trading outpost on Crete. But then the Greek newcomers themselves began to look to the sea. It was an inevitable development, given the nature of their homeland.

Nearly everywhere, the Greeks were surrounded by the sea. Half of their country was interpenetrated by gulfs or scattered as islands far into the Aegean. From almost any point on the mainland shore a Greek mariner could glimpse such islands, stark and mountainous in the clear light, exciting his imagination and inviting him outward. The summer trade winds, blowing steadily from the north, urged him on over the almost tideless waters. An endless succession of promontories and inlets lent shelter from sudden squalls. The summer skies were usually clear, the stars brilliant at night.

To the lure of the sea was added pressure from the land; for the mountainous Greek hinterland was a forbidding and lonely world, inhabited by tough herdsmen living in remote villages. From these mountains a surplus population constantly filtered down to the seaboard, whose narrow but fertile plains produced olives and vegetables, cereals and fruit. As the lowlands in turn became overpopulated, people took to the sea in search of shores and climates like their own. Thus the Greeks expanded east and west, especially between the Eighth and Sixth Centuries B.C.

In Homer's time, the Greeks' knowledge of the greater Mediterranean virtually stopped short at their own western islands. But by 550 B.C. some 250 Greek colonies lined the coasts of the Aegean and the Black Seas, and were scattered far to the south and west as well—to Cyprus, the tip of Libya, Sicily, southern Italy, Corsica, France and even eastern Spain. Greeks, wrote the philosopher Plato, settled the shores of the Mediterranean "like frogs on a pond," turning it into a Greek lake. The Greek names of some of these colonies, thinly disguised, survive: Nice (from *Nicaea*, "Victoria"), Naples (from *Neapolis*, "New town"), Monaco (from a temple to Heracles Monoikos, "Heracles who dwells alone")—to name just a few.

The city-state of Corinth, located on the isthmus linking northern Greece to the Peloponnesian peninsula, was especially prosperous, trading with Asia Minor in one direction and Italy and Sicily in the other. The Corinthians took maximum advantage of their position by constructing a three-mile marine railway across the isthmus: To avoid sailing around the Peloponnesus, cargo vessels were put on wheeled carriages and pulled—probably by oxen—along tracks that were cut into stones laid across the passage.

The colonies were independent of their mother cities in Greece. They maintained cultural and sentimental ties—reverence for Apollo's great shrine at Delphi, participation in the Olympic games—but little else. This combination of spiritual unity and political fragmentation was typical of the Greeks. The mainland itself was dappled with scores of city-states cut off from one another by the mountainous interior and linked largely by sea.

Only in the far western Mediterranean, where Phoenician colonies dominated trade with southern Spain, Sardinia and much of the North African coast, was Greek expansion seriously curtailed. Nonetheless, in about 630 B.C., the mariner Colaeus of Samos, blown by storms the entire length of the Mediterranean, slipped through the Pillars of Hercules undetected by the watchful Phoenicians. He landed at last on the Atlantic coast of Spain. There he sold his pottery to a people who had never before seen Greek products, and at prices that enabled him to return to his homeland a rich man.

A small Phoenician vessel, its bow ornamented by a horse's head, is paddled instead of rowed in an Eighth Century B.C. decoration from a Babylonian palace. Presumably its role on this occasion was to tow the logs seen in the background.

Even the Red Sea and the Indian Ocean were soon to be penetrated by the Greeks; Herodotus records that in about 500 B.C. a Greek sea captain named Scylax traveled overland to India in the service of the Persian King Darius the Great. After navigating the Kabul and Indus Rivers, he cruised along the north shores of the Indian Ocean, rounded the Arabian peninsula, and sailed up into the Red Sea, pioneering a route that would not be more fully charted until the time of Alexander the Great two centuries later.

By 500 B.C. shipbuilding had become a major industry in the dockyards of the Greek city-states. The simple, open galley used by Homer's heroes had now been relegated to light duties in war. As a ship of the line it had been replaced by a sturdier vessel; for the invention of the ram, soon after 1000 B.C., had altered sea warfare profoundly.

No longer were war galleys a means merely of transporting troops for hand-to-hand fighting on deck. Now the ship itself had become an offensive weapon. From its bow, just above the water line, the ram thrust out in a massive bronze-plated snout. The bow was built up in a formidable mass to sustain the shock of impact; the frame, once so frail, was now bolstered by heavy lateral beams and by stout timbers that girdled it horizontally. And some of the newer war galleys were propelled by two ranks of oarsmen, the top rank positioned along the gunwales, the lower one inside the hull. An upper deck, raised upon the first, created a high fighting platform, while lower platforms dominated bow and stern.

By the Sixth Century the standard ship of the line was a galley with 50 oarsmen: 24 per side, plus two steersmen at the stern. Later the oarsmen were arranged in two banks rather than one, so that war galleys measured some 65 feet in length instead of 125 feet, thus presenting a smaller target for ramming. This newer vessel had a straighter prow, and its stern became a decorative, fanlike plume, a flaunted motif that identified the martial role of the vessel. Conquerors took to cutting off these stern ornaments, as well as a galley's rams, and keeping them as trophies of victory.

The merchant galley, too, had developed beyond its Homeric prototype. Now it was high and broad, with rounded stem and stern. Most merchandise was carried by sailing craft; these, although wider, taller and more cumbersome than the war galley, showed graceful concave bows and traveled under a broad square sail. They generally had a shallow draft, so that if no harbor facilities were available, they could be run up onto a beach for unloading.

The design of the merchantman was to remain constant throughout the Fifth Century. But that of the war galley moved ahead dramatically, and within a few years of 500 B.C., the sturdy two-tiered galley was surpassed by a formidable three-level warship, the trireme. By now the entire political aspect of the eastern Mediterranean was changing. A new and bellicose colossus—the Persian Empire—was sprawling westward and threatening to engulf the independent city-states of Greece. To resist the Persian invaders by land invited suicide. So it was to the sea—a turbulent but now familiar friend—that the Greeks were to entrust their salvation.

A legendary mariner's perilous voyage

In Alessandro Allori's version of the Odyssey, Homer's shipwrecked mariner is helped ashore by the goddess Ino.

The most renowned of all ancient mariners is Odysseus, the burly hero of the first great epic of the sea. Although the Greek poet Homer composed the *Odyssey* in the Eighth or Ninth Century B.C., the tale is set almost half a millennium earlier, when the Mediterranean was—even more than in Homer's day—a place of mystery and danger.

In the epic, Odysseus spends 10 years wandering across the sea, a voyage that comes on the heels of a 10-year war against Troy. Perils meet him everywhere, a number of them expressed as mythic embodiments of nautical hazards familiar to seamen of every age: A great whirlpool is characterized as a creature named Charybdis, a surf-beaten cliff as the monster called Scylla. Other dangers are even more imaginative: A one-eyed giant cannibalizes Odysseus' sailors; seductive maidens lure him toward a rocky shoal with beguiling songs; and an island enchantress employs a magic wand to transform his men into swine. Homer also conjured up figures who come to Odysseus' aid—among them, Aeolus, Warden of the Winds, and a benevolent king named Alcinous who provides a ship after the mariner's vessel is destroyed in a storm.

So vivid a tale—beloved by the Greeks and by the Romans after them—inevitably proved an inspiration for artists. Among the most noteworthy visual re-creations of the *Odyssey* is a set of frescoes created in a Florentine palazzo in the 1560s by Alessandro Allori, a literary scholar as well as a painter. He first became interested in the *Odyssey* after reading Dante's assessment of it as "an adventure for adults in search of virtue and knowledge."

The frescoes are a powerful rendition of the tale, but they would have puzzled the ancient Greeks, for Homer's seafaring world bears a startling resemblance to the 16th Century world of the artist. Like many of his contemporaries, Allori was greatly influenced by Michelangelo, and in his scenes such creatures as the one-eyed Cyclops (*pages 34-35*) are as massively masculine as any of Michelangelo's creations. He even anticipates the next century's voluptuous art in such female figures as the maiden princess Nausicaa, who comes upon Odysseus after he is shipwrecked on an island; Allori underscores the romance of the moment and shows her being irresistibly attracted to the mariner.

Allori's Renaissance touches do not detract from the impact of the tale, however, for the *Odyssey* is timeless. Whether in words or in pictures, it stands through the years as a testament not only to the ancient seafarer but also to the ancient sea itself, a realm of mystery and wonder, fear and fantasy, beckoning the adventurers out over the horizon and into the unknown.

A momentous meeting in Homer's epic was that of castaway
Odysseus and the princess Nausicaa. Much of the Odyssey
is a report by the mariner to Nausicaa's father—who then helps
him find his way home. In this scene, the maiden finds
Odysseus in a quiet glade as her helpers play in the background.

In a gory episode, Odysseus and his shipmates, imprisoned in the cave of a one-eyed giant called Cyclops Polyphemus, blind their captor with a smoldering stake. The adventurers managed to slip away from the enraged monster and make their escape on the ship that can be seen beyond the cave entrance.

One of Odysseus' few happy adventures was his visit to
the island of bearded Aeolus, Warden of the Winds, who gave his
guest a bag holding all the world's storms. Allori's version
of the meeting shows Aeolus' sons and daughters whom, Homer
recounted, Aeolus had united in incestuous matrimony.

After encountering giants who sank most of his ships, Odysseus reached the island of the enchantress Circe—and found she used a magic wand to turn men into animals (foreground). In this scene Allori shows the god Hermes giving Odysseus a protective talisman (right) before he meets Circe.

Among Odysseus' most trying encounters were those with the monsters Scylla and Charybdis (below) and the seductive Sirens (opposite). In the first, Allori chooses the moment when Odysseus, attempting to avoid Charybdis' vomited whirlpool (foreground), loses six men to Scylla's devouring jaws.

Warned by Circe of the Sirens' bewitching songs, Odysseus plugged his men's ears, had himself tied to the mast, and thus escaped being lured ashore onto the rocks. Allori outfits the mariners in full armor. The Achaean warriors who were the heroes of Homer's great epic actually wore loincloths.

Chapter 2

An epic clash of East and West

In a theatrical 19th Century rendition of one of history's first great naval battles, Greek and Persian fleets meet off the Aegean island of Salamis in 480 B.C. Atop a cliff at left, Persia's King Xerxes exhorts his admirals as the two flotillas clash and marines assault each other. Xerxes' courtiers cower around him, knowing their cause is lost; even the King's harem ship (lower left) is sinking. The Greek leader Themistocles surveys his triumph from his ship at right, while mist-shrouded gods watch from the sky (upper right) and Poseidon, god of the sea, rises beside Xerxes to point to the impending Persian defeat.

eest thou how God with his lightning smites always the bigger animals, and will not suffer them to wax insolent, while those of a lesser bulk chafe him not? How likewise his bolts fall ever on the highest houses and the tallest trees? So plainly does He love to bring down everything that exalts itself."

Thus, according to the Greek historian Herodotus, did Artabanus, uncle and adviser of the great King Xerxes of Persia, advise his sovereign against tempting divine wrath by invading Greece. At the time—in 485 B.C.—the disparity between the two dominions indeed seemed ludicrous. The Persian Empire stretched as a titanic autocracy from India to Egypt, comprising scores of different states and peoples. Ruled by a quasi-divine king, it was the mightiest empire of its time. Greece, on the other hand, comprised a cluster of quarrelsome city-states. Some of them were governed by a democracy extraordinary for its day, with annually appointed magistrates and assemblies of all citizens. But compared to the feudal hierarchy of the Great King of Persia, this society was hopelessly anarchic. Its colonies, scattered through the Mediterranean, could not coalesce against a Persian assault on the motherland. Of all the Greek states, only Sparta maintained a professional army.

Hostility between Persia and Greece was nothing new. During the reign of Xerxes' father, Darius, the Persians had overwhelmed Greek peoples living in Asia Minor and Cyprus. Then, in 490 B.C., an invading force of 25,000 Persians had landed in the bay of Marathon on the Greek mainland; they had been defeated by the Athenian heavy infantry, but the Persians learned their lesson. Over the next three years the whole Empire was in uproar as Darius prepared a force of men and ships whose like had never been seen. Darius died before he could set this juggernaut in motion, but Xerxes—32 years old when he ascended to the throne in 486—inherited his father's determination to humble Greece. A tall, handsome man, prey to violent passions and childishly intolerant of failure, he was the very model of the Oriental despot—yet he was an able soldier-administrator for all that.

By 483 B.C. hundreds of galleys and transports had been readied in the docks of the Persian Empire—the seafaring cities of Phoenicia, Cyprus, Egypt, and the subject Greek coasts of Asia Minor. Already the Persians commanded the northern Aegean, along whose coast the great army could march. Depots of grain and salted meat were set up along the route; and where the peninsula of Athos lunged into the sea, presenting a dangerous passage for ships, a canal more than a mile in length was dug by forced labor, cutting the neck of the isthmus by the width of two galleys rowing abreast.

More remarkable still was the Persian method of bridging the Hellespont—deep straits, about a mile wide, that separated Asia Minor from Europe. To get his army across, the Great King in early 480 constructed a floating highway—a pair of bridges supported by hundreds of ships meshed side by side. Shortly after the bridges were completed, a violent storm shattered them. Xerxes gave orders that the waters of the Hellespont be scourged with 300 lashes, and that a pair of fetters be thrown into them while the men with the whips cried out: "Thou bitter water, thy

Long-bearded but still a young man
in this portrayal of him as crown prince,
Xerxes succeeded to the throne of the
Persian Empire at the age of 35. After the
Battle of Salamis six years later, his
power gradually eroded, and in 464 B.C.
he was slain by a captain of his guard.

lord lays on thee this punishment because thou hast wronged him without a cause, having suffered no evil at his hands. Verily King Xerxes will cross thee, whether thou wilt or no.''

Herodotus (who was nearly a contemporary of Xerxes) cited this reaction as typical of a barbarian; but the King's action was less a gesture of thwarted megalomania than a magic rite. And now Xerxes ordered that a new, even sturdier pair of bridges be made. Across them were laid flaxen and papyrus cables, topped by a causeway of planks. To keep the horses and pack animals from panicking as they crossed, the boards were strewn with brushwood and compacted soil that would deaden the sound of the hooves, and the swift-flowing waters were screened from sight by makeshift paling. This time the pair of bridges held up.

In the face of such resources and resolve, the Greeks had every reason to view the future with apprehension. A military alliance of Greek states, headed by Sparta and seconded by Athens, could field a dedicated army, but one outnumbered by perhaps 3 to 1. Other Greek states—those along the Persian line of march in the north—had already offered their submission to Xerxes. Still others remained silent or hesitated.

Herodotus recounts that when envoys of Athens approached the oracle of Apollo at Delphi for a favorable omen, they had no sooner stepped into the sanctuary than its priestess, believed to be speaking for the god, threatened them with disaster; their city, said the oracle, would be laid waste by war. Afraid to carry this bitter answer back to Athens, the envoys humbly petitioned the oracle again. This time they were rewarded with a strange but encouraging coda:

> Safe shall the wooden wall continue for thee and thy children.
> Wait not the tramp of the horse, nor the footmen mightily moving
> Over the land, but turn your back to the foe and retire ye.
> Yet shall a day arrive when ye shall meet him in battle.
> Holy Salamis, thou shalt destroy the offspring of women.

There were those in Athens who took ''the wooden wall'' to be the palisades built at the top of the Acropolis, the steep-sided plateau in the city's heart, crowned with shrines to various gods. Others were convinced that the ''wall'' referred to the Athenian fleet, and that the Greeks must meet the Persians on the sea. Among this group was the redoubtable politician Themistocles, an Athenian, probably of modest birth, who had hustled his way into the public eye more than 10 years before as a spokesman for naval rearmament. In 493-492 B.C., this earthy, histrionic but farsighted statesman pushed through the Assembly a motion to fortify Athens' port of Piraeus, five miles from the city's center, with walls so wide that two wagons could travel on them abreast. This work was still unfinished 10 years later, but already the great triple harbor— part naval arsenal, part commercial port—had superseded the old shipbuilding sites on the nearby beaches of Phaleron.

Then, in the winter of 484-483, in the state-owned mines of Laurium, southeast of Athens, a huge vein of silver was discovered. Within a year it had yielded two and a half tons of the precious metal. Themistocles seized on this providential bounty and, against heavy opposition, persuaded the Assembly to allocate the money to the construction of warships. On the eroded hills of the little city-state, lumber was scarce and often of poor quality, but Athens brought in timber from abroad, especially from the pine forests of Macedon to the north. For three years after 483, the shipwrights of Piraeus and Phaleron, working at full speed, launched as many as six war galleys every month. By the winter of 481-480, new crews were being recruited and trained, and more ropes and sails were being imported.

The 50-oared galley of the previous century had by now given way to the classic fighting ship of the ancient Greek world: the trireme. In these vessels (whose name means "three-fitted") nearly everything was sacrificed to speed and mobility. Some 170 rowers, arranged in three superimposed lines along either side of the ship, pulled at oars as long as 14 feet. So low was the galley—a mere eight and a half feet above the water line—that the bottom rank of rowers labored on oars projecting through ports only 18 inches above the waves; in rough weather they stopped up the ports with leather bags. The top rank of rowers sat on benches raised above the gunwales and rested their oars on outriggers two feet wide.

These great ships measured 120 feet in length, 10 times their width. The ram at their prows had now flowered into three prongs, and the stern curled inward like a tall, graceful fan. In battle they left most of their sails ashore and carried only a small one for emergencies; it was stowed out of the way as they went into action. Powered by oars, they resembled enormous sea centipedes.

The trireme was a warship par excellence. It was constructed for short, fierce bouts, not for long campaigns, and it was far from seaworthy. Looking more like a racing shell than an offshore vessel, it was so light that between periods of duty it was taken out of the water and suspended on racks in the sheds of the navy bases. To support its lightweight skeleton and its thin hull during a storm, the trireme was rigged with a cable extending from stem to stern. Yet whole fleets of triremes foundered when caught by gales.

The Greek trireme's oarsmen were generally poor citizens of the city-state, or rowers hired from other parts of the Greek world. Besides the oarsmen, the trireme usually carried a basic marine force of some 14 spearmen and four archers, with 30 sailors and officers. The captaincy of a war galley was often a political appointment, so the running of the ship generally devolved on the executive officer, called the *kybernetes*, or "helmsman." Beneath him ranked the *proreus* (lookout), the officer commanding the foredeck. Another officer, called the *keleustes* (time beater), set the tempo for the oarsmen—although a flutist, often a slave, maintained the beat when it had been established. The fifth and lowest-ranking commissioned officer, the *pentecontarchos*, served as paymaster and administrative drudge. And beneath these five were 25 highly trained sailors, including the all-important ship's carpenter.

The trireme's tactics were those of ramming and boarding. Some city-states, such as Corinth, favored a heavy galley whose wide decks could carry a larger force of marines. Others, like Athens, preferred fast, easily handled vessels that disabled their opponents with the ram. Two maneuvers in particular were employed on the sea. The *diecplus* (sail

Bridging the Hellespont with a tethered fleet

A major obstacle in the path of the Persian King Xerxes' army was the Hellespont, a waterway at the head of the Aegean that was nearly a mile wide at its narrowest and separated Asia Minor from Europe. Xerxes bridged the gap with ships, not in a ferrying operation but by constructing a unique pair of bridges with hundreds of vessels ranged side by side.

The 120-foot-long ships were lashed together parallel to the banks of the Hellespont. "Having joined the vessels," wrote the Greek historian Herodotus, the bridgebuilders "moored them with anchors of unusual size," in order to resist the strong currents and the winds that blew through the Hellespont. The Persians then strung cables of papyrus and flax (the latter so stout that they weighed 50 pounds per foot) across the floating vessels from bank to bank, and windlasses on both beaches winched the cables taut. Next, Herodotus reports, planks "were laid side by side upon the tightened cables" and fastened in place.

Xerxes' engineers, in short, built a combination suspension and pontoon bridge. The cables took some of the weight and provided more consistent stability than the separate vessels, and the ships kept the lengthy, heavy cables from sagging into the water.

Atop the planks of this combination bridge, soil was packed down to make an earthen roadway for the cavalry and troops. Walls made of matted branches (cut away in the drawing below to show the ships) were built to conceal the Hellespont so that Xerxes' horses would not panic.

Xerxes built two of these bridges, using 360 ships to cross a stretch a mile and a quarter wide and 314 vessels at a narrower crossing nearby. So gigantic was his army that its horses tramped across the two highways for a week.

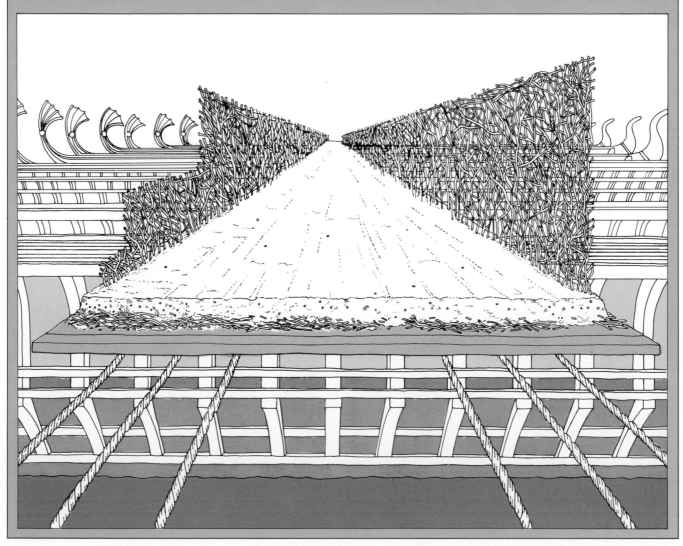

through) was a concerted attack that involved penetrating the enemy's line, then turning to ram his flanks and sterns. The *periplus* (sail around) outflanked or enveloped him, then assailed him in the rear.

The army and navy of Xerxes began to cross the Hellespont in early May of 480. Incense was burned on the floating bridges at dawn, and myrtle boughs were strewn about to bring good fortune to the enterprise. Many men had been mustered; Herodotus inflated the number to a fantastic two million and said that they drank whole rivers dry. Probably they numbered about 200,000—still a prodigious force for the time—attended by a multitude of porters and pack animals.

Their march was slow and magnificent. The baggage train led the way, protected by many divisions of infantry, an exotic mélange from all corners of the Persian Empire. Then came a thousand of Persia's finest cavalry and another thousand picked footmen, marching with spears reversed. Next, drawn by 18 powerful horses, rolled the chariot of Ormazd, supreme god of the Persians—a sacred and empty vehicle whose driver walked behind it, holding the reins, "for no mortal," wrote Herodotus, "is ever allowed to mount into the car."

The chariot of Xerxes himself came next, followed by the flower of Persian infantry and cavalry and, behind these favored troops, the mass of lesser infantry levied from all over the Empire—scimitar-wielding warriors from the Caspian Sea, Mesopotamians with iron-studded cudgels, Indians with bows and arrows, Ethiopians wearing horses' scalps complete with ears and mane. These made up the bulk of Xerxes' army.

For seven days they poured across the double bridge. They then turned west and began to move irresistibly along the northern coast of the Aegean. Beside them, cutting the sea with serried oars, went the imperial fleet—as huge and heterogeneous as the army. The Persians themselves were an almost landlocked people, and had no navy. They relied for their fleet on the ancient seagoing peoples of their Empire. The skilled mariners and fast war galleys of the Phoenicians, Egyptians, Cypriotes and the Greeks of Asia Minor had gathered into a great force of more than 1,200 triremes, with countless other warships, transports and supply vessels in support. The whole sea power of the eastern Mediterranean, in fact, was thrusting across the Aegean against Greece.

The attackers' triremes, like those of the Greeks, carried some 170 oarsmen as well as sailors and fighting marines. In the huge flotilla, the 300 vessels of the Phoenicians were the largest and most nimble, yet they were less sturdy for ramming than Greek vessels, since the Phoenicians' tactics concentrated on boarding the enemy. The Phoenician crews wore bronze helmets and breastpieces of stout linen, carried light, rimless shields and wielded javelin-like spears. The Cypriote contingent numbered perhaps 150; its men wore light armor and were equipped with swords and spears. The 200-odd Egyptian ships held more formidable men—heavy infantry in metal-plated helmets, with broad-rimmed shields, long spears and hefty axes. They were to prove an ugly foe. Other parts of the Empire had contributed about 250 assorted vessels.

Finally, Persia's Greek and Asia Minor confederates had mustered nearly 300 triremes. Their crews were mostly trained and armed like the

Drying sheds for Athens' galleys

Like all warships of the day, Athens' galleys were thin-skinned vessels light enough to be hauled from the sea by manpower alone—and frequent hauling out was necessary to prevent them from becoming waterlogged and sluggish. While on duty, they were dragged onto the beach every night. And between missions the galleys were stored in sheds that had been built expressly for them in Piraeus, the city-state's port (pages 48-49).

These sheds were formidably solid, with slipways carved out of bedrock and walls built of stone blocks. The interior was partitioned by stone columns that allowed maximum ventilation and efficient drying of the galleys. The buildings were roofed in pairs—one pitched roof covering two sheds (opposite)—and were grouped in long lines along the waterfront. During the Fourth Century B.C., there were at least 372 of these ship sheds, as they were called, in Piraeus' three harbors.

The galleys, hauled into the buildings stern first, were held upright in their berths either by a wooden frame or by a special groove carved into the stone foundations to secure the keel. The mast was unstepped and stored alongside or in racks above the vessel, and the sails and rigging were taken to another storehouse, known as the Arsenal.

During their stay on land the warships were guarded against fire and sabotage by a force of as many as 500 troops, and their care was supervised by a special board of overseers, who checked the gear for each vessel as it was hauled out and again on the day it was refloated. When the proud, privileged vessels slipped back into the harbor and began another tour of duty, the leaders of Athens' Assembly often would gather on the jetty to see them off.

Drying out between missions, three Athenian war galleys poke their prows from their sheds along Piraeus' waterfront. Each of the specially built sheds was 120 feet long and 20 feet wide.

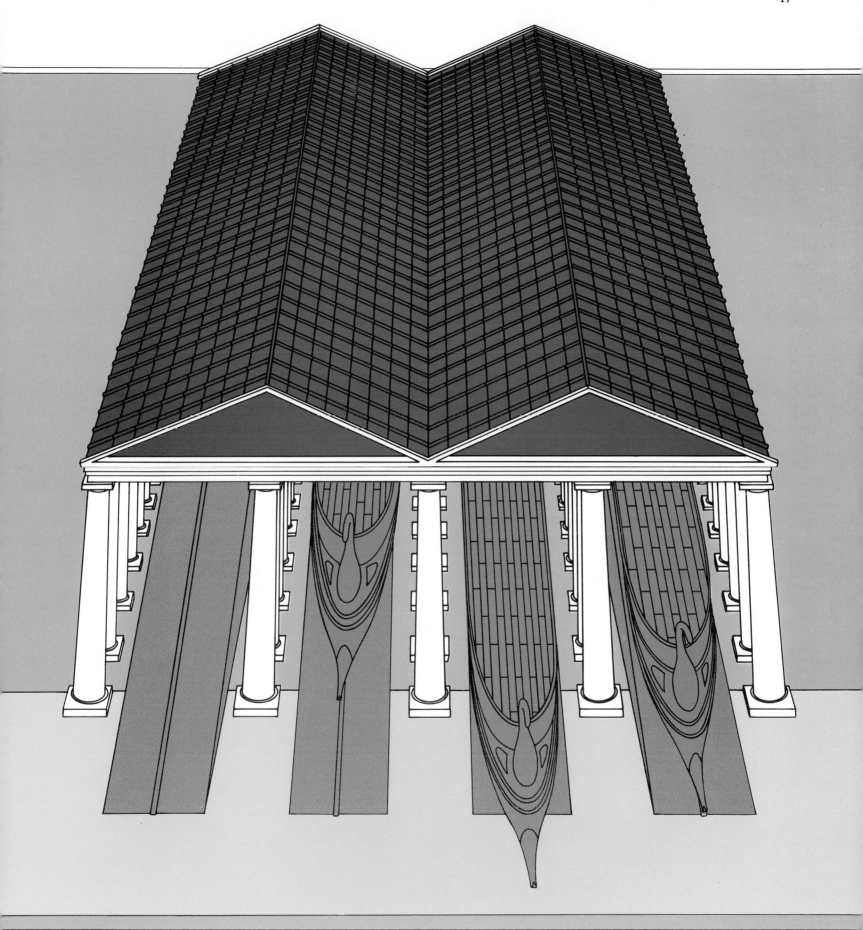

The great triple-harbor complex of Piraeus was dominated in the Fifth and Fourth Centuries B.C. by the Athenian navy. Kantharas, the main harbor (right), was lined on its longest side with warehouses for commercial shipping; but adjacent to these, along the right shore of the harbor, were several dozen sheds for war galleys. The two other harbors, Munichia (far left) and Zea (center) were entirely military in function. Zea was the major naval base, with sheds for 196 galleys; behind the sheds opposite its entrance was the Arsenal, a long gray building (page 50) where the galleys' rigging was stored. Piraeus was a

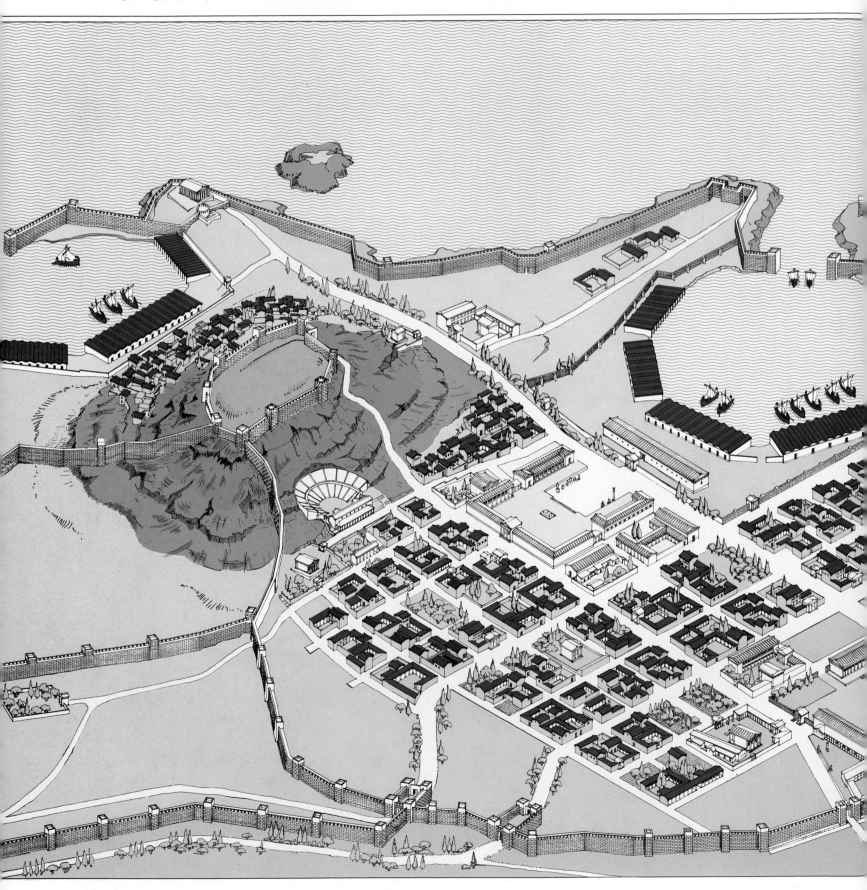

small city in itself, supposedly designed by the first known city planner, Hippodamus. Besides its stores and houses, Piraeus had an open square (across the avenue running past Zea's Arsenal) and two shell-shaped open theaters. The whole complex was surrounded by a high wall, built of heavy limestone and intermittently topped by defensive towers; the walls protruded into each harbor so as to leave only a narrow entrance that could be closed with chains. Piraeus' walls extended in a corridor (lower left) all the way to Athens, forming a secure, six-mile passageway from the city to its formidable naval headquarters.

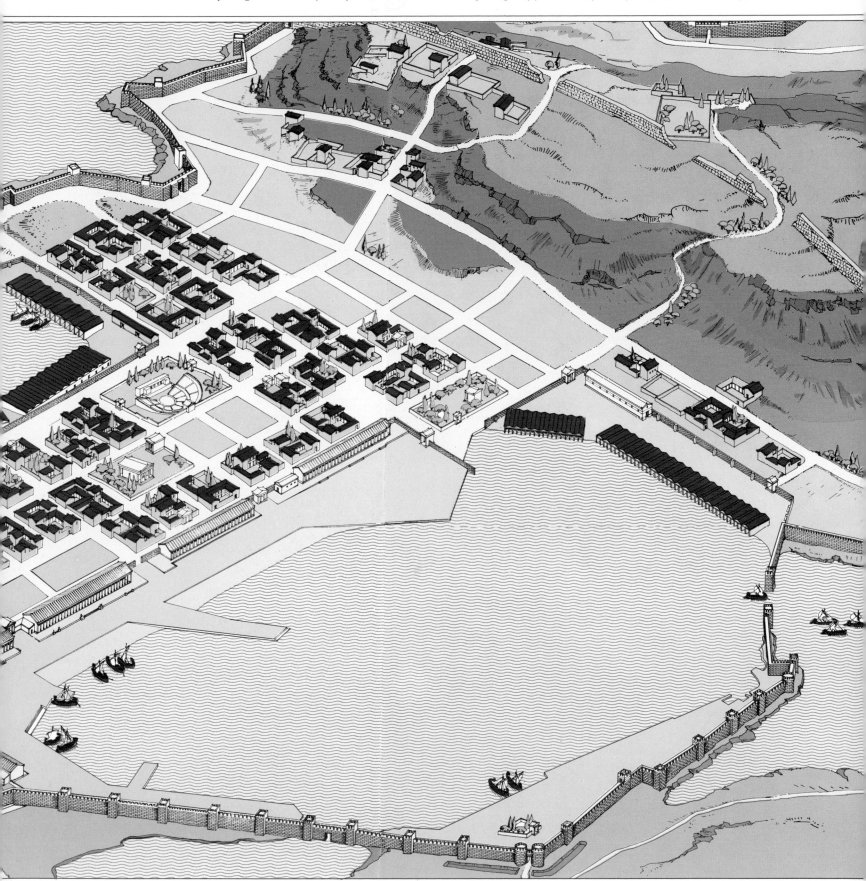

While war galleys dried out in Piraeus, gear was kept in the Arsenal (below), a massive building 425 feet long and 60 feet wide. Along each side of its central aisle were compartments (cutaway, at right below) for storing sails and rigging. The loft above the main aisle offered additional storage space; equipment was lifted there with the aid of block and tackle. The Arsenal was constructed of marble quarried near Athens.

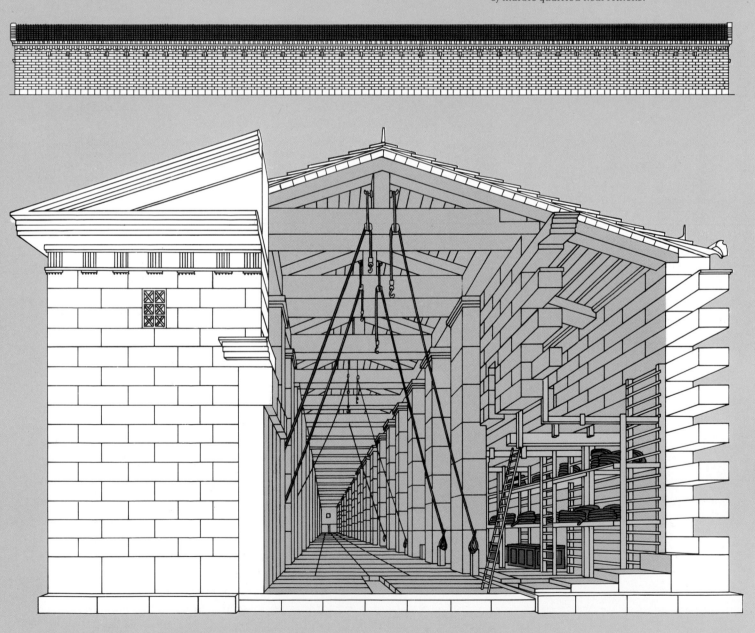

western Greeks—heavily and well—but a few sported outlandish idio-syncrasies: goatskin cloaks and hats stuck with feathers. The most con-spicuous group—five ships from the kingdom of Halicarnassus on the western shore of Asia Minor—was led by a woman, Queen Artemisia, whose "brave spirit and manly daring," wrote Herodotus, "sent her forth to the war when no need required her to adventure."

In all this variform fleet, few but the Phoenicians could be trusted to remain loyal to Persia. Egypt, Cyprus and the Greek states of Ionia had all rebelled against the Empire within living memory, and it may have been because of this that their ships each carried some 30 Persian marines. These warrior watchmen, dressed in trousers, felt hats or turbans, and linen tunics, were armed not only with the Persian national weapon, a bow with a range of some 120 yards, but also with a short spear, a dagger and a circular shield.

Against the oncoming 1,200 ships, the Greeks could muster about 450 triremes of their own; of these, more than half were from Athens—fruit of Themistocles' wisdom and the silver mines of Laurium. But to man them, the city-state must embark all its 20,000 men of fighting age and relinquish the land war to her allies, leaving Athens almost defenseless.

Yet this was what Themistocles persuaded the Athenians to do. He realized that the double threat of the Persian advance by land and sea would have to be met on both land and sea; but he envisioned the army's role as merely a holding operation, while the real issue was to be fought out on the water. Neither the military aristocracy of Sparta nor Athenian conservatives, appalled at the idea of abandoning their city, agreed with him. The navy, in any case, had always been considered inferior to the army. But the shadow of Xerxes, falling huge across the whole country, turned the tide of opinion in Themistocles' favor.

The Greeks were fired by a terrible patriotism. Their homes, their gods, the very spirit of their lives—democratic freedom in its precious infancy—were threatened by the dead hand of Persian despotism, a world of divine autocracy in which a man was no more than a slave to his king or his god. So the Athenians put their trust at last in the "wooden walls" of their galleys, and by late July the whole working male popula-tion of the little city-state, slave and free, had taken to the sea.

By now the Persian army had turned the head of the Aegean and was marching south unopposed. In its path, the states of northeastern Greece submitted without a blow, and soon Xerxes' vanguard was moving un-der the shadow of Mount Olympus, barely 160 miles from Athens. The Greeks had once thought of facing the Persians in this region, but no good narrow pass existed for their stand, and the coast offered the Greek fleet only open waters and a dangerously craggy and harborless shore. Eventually the Greek army—an assemblage of land forces from many city-states—decided to make a stand where the mountains fell steeply to the sea at the rocky defile of Thermopylae, 85 miles from Athens, while the Greek fleet, mainly Athenian, planned to meet the Persian ships in the waters of Artemisium to the northeast. Behind the defending fleet the 110-mile-long island of Euboea, hugging the coast, offered a safe channel for withdrawal, with friendly shores on either side.

But the Greek fleet that sailed north was pitifully small. A reserve flotilla of almost 200 ships had to be left behind to guard the shores to the south. So now, against more than 1,200 Persian war galleys, the Greeks advanced with only 271 ships. Of these, 147 were Athenian, including 100 of Themistocles' new triremes. Most of the rest were sent by Athens' allies in the Peloponnesus.

Within two days they reached Artemisium, at the head of the island of Euboea, and hauled their galleys up on its long, shallow beach. Here they awaited the Persians. They set up beacons on the hills and on the island of Skiathos to the north, where several galleys kept watch. Some 40 miles to their west, on the mainland, a 7,000-man advance force of the army had reached the pass of Thermopylae. This little vanguard, led by King Leonidas of Sparta but predominately composed of soldiers from the Peloponnesus, probably hoped to hold the pass until a larger army could march north at the end of the month. Meanwhile, they dug in and built a heavy wall across the throat of the defile. Then they too waited. A trusted Athenian officer named Habronichus, captaining a fast, 30-oared galley, was the sole liaison between the fleet and the army.

At dawn on August 3, thirteen fast Phoenician galleys—harbingers of the Persian fleet—swept down on the Greeks' advance patrol at Ski-athos. A reconnaissance unit of three Greek triremes fled before them, but one by one they were overhauled. The Phoenicians meted out a quixotic treatment to their captives. From the first captured vessel they took the most handsome Greek soldier and cut his throat as a ritual sacrifice. On the second, a Greek marine named Pytheas, who fought with furious valor before falling, was nursed back to health with the aid of the Phoenician ship's medicine chest (something unknown to the Greeks) and exhibited with admiration to the rest of the fleet. The third vessel ran aground, and its crew escaped into the hinterland.

Unhampered now, the Phoenicians prepared the way for the main Persian force. They set up a stone marker to warn their cohorts away from the reef between Skiathos and the mainland, reconnoitered the generous harbor of nearby Aphetae for a naval base, and surveyed the Greek fleet as it lay opposite them on the sandy fringes of Euboea. By August 12 the armada of the Great King was sprawling along the coasts close to the north. By night its foremost ships were hauled onto the beaches; the rest of the fleet rode eight deep at anchor offshore. To the Greeks, staring north, the whole country seemed to be covered by the sparks of the enemy's fires, and the sea dotted with their riding lights.

The oracle at Delphi was visited again and told the panicking inquirers: "Pray to the winds." On the morning of August 13, Greek prayers were answered: A savage storm erupted out of the calm. Referring to the god of the north wind, Herodotus wrote: "Boreas fell with violence on the barbarians at their anchorage." The Greeks retreated deeper into their channel and waited while for three days the storm lashed the exposed Persian fleet, driving scores of triremes onto the rocks, where they were smashed or sunk. The Persian crews, floundering ashore, barricaded themselves from the local inhabitants behind the debris of their ships. All around them the beaches became littered with a horrific richness of Persian treasure amid bloated corpses. Some 400 triremes vanished as if they had never existed.

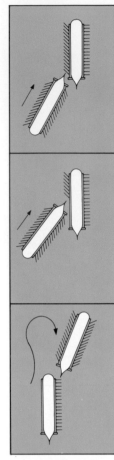

Tactics with the trireme often involved disabling the enemy before going for the kill. If there was enough room between the galleys, a captain might perform the maneuver called a diecplus (sail through). Approaching at an angle (1), the attacker tried to sideswipe the enemy with his ram and sweep away the defender's oars (2). He then backed off from his maimed foe, rounded him and rammed him from astern (3).

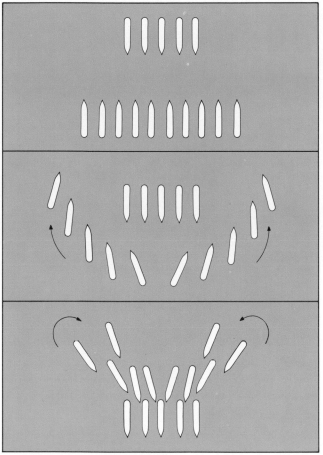

To counter the diecplus, the defending naval commander might move his galleys so close together (1) that the attacker would be unable to slip through. But this move could be dangerous if the enemy badly outnumbered his force, as here. The attacker could execute another maneuver called the periplus (sail around), encircling the defending squadron (2) and bringing his rams against the defenders' vulnerable sterns (3).

Not until the morning of August 16 did the gale let up—perhaps because Xerxes' priests, wrote Herodotus, lulled the wind with spells—"or perhaps," he added with a dash of Greek skepticism, "it ceased of itself." The crippled fleet straggled into its base at Aphetae for repairs. Yet it still outnumbered the Greeks by about 3 to 1; and many Greek commanders talked of abandoning Artemisium and retreating south.

The first night after the storm, 200 Persian galleys and supply vessels set off south around the eastern coast of Euboea, intending to circle the island and block the Greeks' escape from the rear. On a given signal, the main Persian fleet at Aphetae would push forward in a massed frontal attack, and the two fleets would crush their enemy between them.

This ambitious plan might have spelled the end for the Greeks had it not been betrayed to Themistocles by a deserter, a diver named Scyllias, who crossed the strait to Artemisium from Aphetae to warn the Greeks (Herodotus says that Scyllias claimed to have swum underwater for 10 miles without surfacing; the fact is, says the historian, he probably swam normally to Artemisium, or even rowed). The report of Persian plans and numbers sent such fear through the Greek chiefs that Themistocles had to bribe and browbeat them into obedience. At all events, the Greeks decided to attack before they were sandwiched.

"When the Persian commanders and crews saw the Greeks thus sailing toward them with their few ships," wrote Herodotus, "they thought them possessed with madness, and went out to meet them," confident of easy victory. But the Greeks had advanced suddenly, late in the afternoon, and the Persian squadrons, still refurbishing, were strung out all along the coast. So unexpected was the attack that most of the first line of Persian war galleys fell to the Greeks. But the Persians soon came swarming out from their many anchorages and began to surround the attackers. With every minute, as ship after ship arrived, the Greek advantage faded. Finally, the Greeks fell back into a defensive formation. Side by side, their heavy ships presented to the Persians a huge defensive arc. Herodotus recorded that the arc became a "hedgehog" formation, called the *kyklos* (circle): The beleaguered ships lay with sterns inward and bows outward—a gigantic circle of bronze rams and armed men.

Against this formation, in the dimming light, the Persians could make no headway. Despite superior numbers, they could not break through the arc. The Greeks were heavily armed, their bronze helmets plumed with horsehair and their cheeks ringed with protective plates, lending their faces an almost mineral inhumanity. Bronze cuirasses protected their chests and backs. Their legs were sheathed in bronze greaves. Holding three-foot round or violin-shaped shields and wielding spears and iron-bladed swords, they were terrible in defense.

At dusk the Persians broke off, and each fleet retired to its base. That night another storm broke. Corpses and wreckage, Greek and Persian alike, drifted up to Aphetae, bumping against the anchored ships in the night, fouling the oars of those on guard and unnerving the sailors, while thunder crashed over Mount Pelion to the north. At the same time, the 200-vessel Persian fleet that was rounding the southern tip of Euboea took the full force of the storm. Some of the ships were dashed on the rocks. Others fled before the wind and were scattered.

Preliminary movements along a convoluted coastline

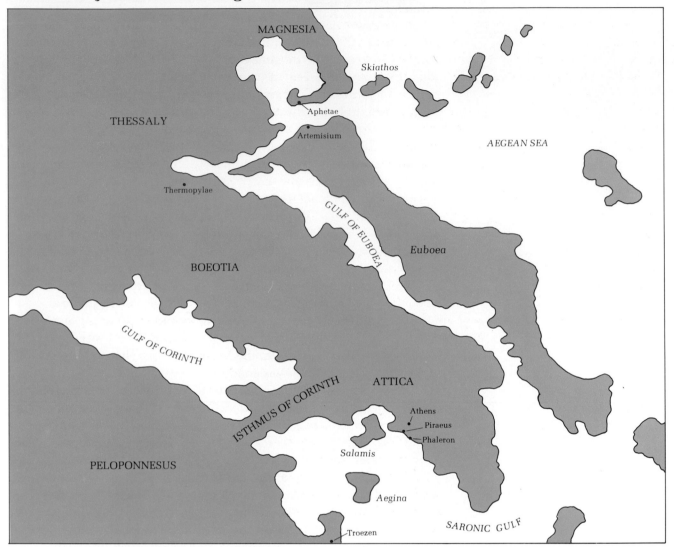

By August 19, both by land and sea, the campaign had reached its crux. Just as the Greek fleet had been holding the Persians at bay in the channel at Artemisium, so the Greek army had been blocking Xerxes' armies in the pass of Thermopylae. But now, after two days of heroic defense, the Greek flank had been turned by a traitor who had led the Persians over a path through the hills to the south. The bulk of the Greek army retreated while it could save itself, leaving Leonidas with 2,000 men to hold the pass and delay the Persian advance as long as possible.

On the morning of August 20, the Persians attacked overwhelmingly by land and sea. At Thermopylae, Leonidas and his battalion fought with a valor that has enshrined them ever since in a glow of heroism. At the last moment, before the Persians finally overcame them, Habronichus' galley slipped anchor and sailed for Artemisium to warn the fleet. By midday the battle at Thermopylae was over. The way to Athens lay open.

With Habronichus still en route to Artemisium, Themistocles was ignorant of the fate of the army. And his fleet was bracing for the enemy

With Athens threatened, Greek warships went north through the Gulf of Euboea and confronted the Persian invaders off Artemisium (top center). Although outnumbered 2 to 1, the Greeks fought the Persians to a standoff, then retreated south through the gulf. The Persians followed, setting the stage for the battle off Salamis (bottom center).

advance by sea. In the bright August sunlight, the Persians came in a massive concave crescent, the flanks straining forward to envelop the Greek line. But the Greek ships, their force bolstered by 53 new galleys from Attica, stretched from one shore of the Gulf of Euboea to the other and could not be surrounded. They confronted the Persians calmly, head on. The two lines crashed together. The bronze-headed rams tore at the opposing bows; but after the first splintering impact, the battle stagnated into a turmoil of interlocked decks, with the marines pressing from ship to ship as if on land, slashing and thrusting their way through crowds of unarmed oarsmen. The Egyptian soldiers proved especially dangerous: Wielding boarding spears and poleaxes, they took a terrible toll of the Greeks. By nightfall half the Athenian vessels and many Persian galleys were disabled; they had fought each other to a standstill.

At dusk the Persians retired to Aphetae, while the Greeks, wandering over the straits, picked up their drowned comrades and tried to salvage half-sunk ships. On the beach of Artemisium, the flames from burning wreckage and funeral pyres filled the night with a bitter brightness. And now Habronichus' galley arrived with the news of the massacre at Thermopylae. The fleet could afford to wait no longer. Leaving their fires burning on the shore to persuade the Persians that they still held position, the Greeks sailed down the long Gulf of Euboea under cover of darkness, back to their threatened homeland.

But the battles at Artemisium had not been in vain. The Greeks had faced up to Xerxes' navy. They were "taught by actual achievements in the face of danger," wrote the Greek historian Plutarch, "that neither multitudes of ships nor brilliantly decorated figureheads nor boastful shouts nor barbarous battle hymns have any terror for men who know how to come to close quarters and dare to fight there." And the gods seemed to be on their side. By storm as well as combat the Persians had suffered cruelly. At Artemisium, wrote the poet Pindar, "the brave sons of Athens planted the shining cornerstone of their freedom."

Only the cornerstone, however, and not yet the structure of freedom. Indeed, to Xerxes it now seemed that Greece lay at his feet. Marching south and inland from Thermopylae, his army sacked those cities that had not surrendered, while the battle fleet sailed down the Gulf of Euboea, ravaging the coasts.

The terror of Xerxes' name, and the news of Thermopylae, preceded him. South of Athens, the Peloponnesian Greeks, with an army of 30,000, were building a wall across the isthmus of their great peninsula, abandoning Athens to its fate. Themistocles, limping back home with his fleet, found Athens in turmoil. In two days the Persians would reach the suburbs. Many Athenians were fleeing in panic—yet thousands more were unwilling to leave their city. Indeed, wrote Plutarch, "most of them were distressed at the thought, saying that they neither wanted victory nor understood what safety could mean if they abandoned to the enemy the shrines of their gods and the sepulchers of their fathers."

Themistocles ordered compulsory evacuation of all residents except the old and sick. For two days the sea was covered with ships as the populace was ferried to the nearby city-states of Troezen and Aegina or to Salamis, an island four miles west of the city, where the fleet head-

Climax at Salamis

In the use of land features, the Battle of Salamis was a brilliant example of naval strategy. The Greek defenders, who were massed along Salamis' eastern coast (*inset map*), were outnumbered 3 to 1 by the attacking Persian fleet. Their chief naval strategist, Themistocles, therefore refused to be lured into the open waters of the Saronic Gulf, where the Persians lay in wait. Instead, he decided to make a stand in the narrow Salamis channel.

To entice the Persians into the channel, he pretended to be a turncoat and transmitted false intelligence to the Persians that the Greeks were about to scatter and escape. King Xerxes quickly dispatched squadrons to cut off the presumptive escape route through the Megarian channel west of the Bay of Eleusis. And early in the morning of September 20, 480, Xerxes sent his main fleet up past the island of Psyttaleia and into the Salamis channel, thus sealing off the only other avenue of escape. Having heard reports that the Greek admirals were already demoralized, he believed they would quickly surrender when they realized that they were trapped.

It was the Persian fleet, however, that sailed into the trap. Instead of fleeing, or even awaiting their attackers in the wider waters of the Bay of Eleusis, the Greek ships confronted the Persian war galleys as they filed through the narrow passageway between Aghios Giorgios Island and an island close to the mainland. The southward-looking view here shows the climactic point in the battle, just after the two opposing fleets have come together. The Persian vanguard has crowded through the bottleneck and has begun to fan out; these few advance Persian galleys are under attack by the main body of the Greek fleet. Behind the entranceway, working their way up past Psyttaleia and waiting their turn to file into the Salamis channel, most of the Persian fleet is still out of action, with the exception of their left flank, which is under attack by a squadron of Greek ships from Salamis harbor (*middle right*).

What Themistocles accomplished in one stroke was to turn the Greeks' numerical inferiority into a tactical superiority, with most of the Greek warships positioned so they could concentrate on a few Persian ships at a time as these emerged through the bottleneck. The overpowered Persians fought gamely for nearly an hour, until it became obvious that they would be slaughtered piecemeal. When the Persian vanguard turned to retreat, their galleys plowed into the main body of the Persian fleet crowding into the channel. Of 1,000 Persian attackers, 200 in the advance wave were smashed or sunk, and hundreds more were captured or destroyed in retreat.

BAY OF ELEUSIS

MEGARIAN CHANNEL

Aghios Giorgios

Mount
Aigaleos

SALAMIS CHANNEL

Salamis

ISLAND
OF
SALAMIS

Psyttaleia

SARONIC GULF

N
W · E
S

quarters lay. Hundreds of deserted dogs gathered on the shores and howled after the departing boats. On the Acropolis towering above, a skeleton garrison, along with the priestesses who tended the shrines, stood behind the wooden barricades protecting the sacred heights. They were determined to make a suicide stand.

On August 27, as the Persian vanguard clattered into the city's empty streets, the last Greek ship was crossing the sea to Salamis. Now everything depended on the fleet. But its leaders, meeting in council, were still divided. Some, notably the Peloponnesians, wanted to fall back on the isthmus. Others, including Themistocles and the Athenians, urged that the Persian fleet be met at Salamis. While they continued to debate, Greek sailors staring over the sea watched a pall of smoke rising from the Acropolis. Soon afterward they learned that the Persians had destroyed its wooden ramparts with flaming arrows, and that when their forces had scaled its heights the defenders either had committed suicide by hurling themselves from the cliffs or had been butchered—soldiers and priestesses alike.

In the fleet some captains were so alarmed that they proposed immediate flight westward. But Themistocles continued to argue that the fleet should hold its station. Salamis, he pointed out, was both tactically and strategically more favorable to the Greeks than the isthmus. Like the island of Euboea, it hugged the Greek mainland and provided only narrow entrances into the long channel between. Such a confined front favored the fewer but heavier Greek ships. If they defeated the enemy here, a Persian attack on the Peloponnesus would not be feasible.

The Corinthian admiral, Adeimantus, told Themistocles to hold his tongue, that he was now a man without a country. Themistocles furiously retorted that Athens had 200 warships, which was country enough. "For the whole fortune of the war," he declared to Eurybiades, the commander in chief, "depends on our ships. Be thou persuaded by my words." To his plea he added a threat: "We will take our families on board and go, just as we are, to Siris, in Italy. You then, when you have lost allies like us, will hereafter call to mind what I have now said."

The argument continued for three weeks, while Xerxes assembled his naval might on the captured beaches of Phaleron, and the Greeks waited uneasily in the anchorages of Salamis. For the time being, it was a stalemate. The Persians were reluctant to attack in closed waters. But they could not advance on the Peloponnesus while the Greek fleet remained intact. The Greek losses at Artemisium had partly been made good by a reserve flotilla of 99 ships—57 of them Athenian—and the battle fleet now numbered 310 war galleys. The Persians had brought up their own reserves to replace their losses at Artemisium; they had now some 1,000 ships and again outnumbered the Greeks by more than 3 to 1. But they were so wary of engaging those powerful galleys and bronze-sheathed men that Xerxes first attempted to build a causeway between the mainland and Salamis—a distance of three quarters of a mile across a sea that was in places more than three fathoms deep. But the Greeks brought up a regiment of archers who harassed the construction teams with such deadly effect that the project was abandoned.

By about September 16, Xerxes' patience was giving out. He came

down to Phaleron, wrote Herodotus, and called a naval conference to debate "whether a sea fight should be risked or no." His commanders, seated below him in order of state, urged him to attack—all but Artemisia, Queen of Halicarnassus, who counseled him to march on the Peloponnesus so that the Peloponnesian contingents in the Greek fleet would be drawn away to defend their homeland and Greek unity would be shattered. But the majority won the day. By evening the Persian fleet had sailed for Salamis and had taken up its battle stations. Xerxes, however, also took Queen Artemisia's advice to the extent of sending some 30,000 men, carrying torches and singing battle songs, along the road to the isthmus, hoping to lure the Peloponnesian flotillas into the open sea.

Even the awesome spectacle of the advancing Persian fleet did not resolve the dispute among the Greek commanders, who still debated where to make their stand. One group, wrote Herodotus, argued that "it

A white-gowned Queen Artemisia of Halicarnassus (right), commanding a squadron in the Persian fleet, sees that the struggle at Salamis is lost and breaks away, sinking one of her own ships in the process (foreground). The 19th Century painter of this scene erroneously fitted out the fleet with tower-topped masts, not in use until centuries after the battle.

A fighting force girded in bronze

Every bit as deadly as the battering rams used by the Greek war galleys at the Battle of Salamis were the marines that were massed on the galleys' fighting decks. They boarded enemy vessels wielding long spears or murderous swords, and they wore the finest armor of their day.

A Greek warrior of the Fifth Century B.C.—whether he was a foot soldier on land or a marine on a galley's deck—was virtually encased in bronze, from close-fitting leg greaves to a helmet with nose and cheek guards (center). Even the decorative plumes on top of the Greek helmet were intended to serve a protective purpose: They cushioned the shock of an enemy's overhand blow. A shield made of wood reinforced with bronze helped to guard the warrior's body from chin to knee.

The Persian fighting men, by contrast, were attired in cloth helmets and leather corselets and carried woven-wicker shields and shorter spears. Many also were armed with ornate and lethal daggers (page 62). But so pronounced was the Greek advantage in equipment that the Persian marines did not often survive to get within dagger range.

A bronze statuette from the late Sixth Century B.C. preserves all the equipment used by a Greek warrior except the spear that his arm is cocked to thrust.

A Greek war helmet (right) includes a narrow nose guard as well as protection for the cheeks and the back of the neck.

Nearly full protection is provided by this set of Greek armor, with full face guard, cuirass for the upper torso and a section to cover the wearer's abdomen.

was best to sail to the Peloponnesus and risk battle for that, instead of abiding at Salamis and fighting for a land already taken by the enemy.''

In the end Themistocles forced matters to a head. This blunt and ostentatious man was yet a subtle manipulator of men's minds. He secretly dispatched his trusted slave Sicinnus in a small boat across the sea to Xerxes. Sicinnus probably left in the darkness before dawn on September 19 and reached the Persians at first light. He told them that he had come from Themistocles, who had changed sides and was ready to join the Persians. The Greeks, he said, were planning flight, and if Xerxes attacked now, he would annihilate his enemies before they evaded him.

Some scholars doubt this story. But whether or not Xerxes did receive such a message, he sent his fleet into action on the night of September 19. His first moves were preparatory. Some 400 soldiers were silently landed on the islet of Psyttaleia, south of the Salamis channel. Meanwhile the powerful Egyptian squadron secretly circled Salamis and blocked the channel's western exit. The straits to either side were covered by other units of the Persian fleet. The Greeks were now trapped and forcibly united. Themistocles had won his way.

All night the Persian squadrons patrolled the exits of the channel, awaiting the Greek flight. Around them the harsh shores and calm sea were lighted by a full moon. Hour after hour, the great fleet—arrayed two deep around the isle of Psyttaleia—gazed across at the enemy warships. The Greek galleys did not move.

Themistocles, Herodotus reports, addressed his men at daybreak. He "contrasted what was noble with what was base," Herodotus wrote, and bade them "always to make choice of the nobler part." As dawn spread over the sky, the men embarked and the ships pushed out to sea.

Precisely how the crucial battle was joined is unknown. But it is clear that the Greeks simulated flight in order to draw the Persians deeper into the narrows. The Corinthian squadron of 50 made a feint to the north, and the whole Greek fleet, wrote Herodotus, "began to back water." Momentarily it must have seemed to the Persians that the Greeks were indeed starting to flee. The Persians came pressing into the narrows.

An 18-inch Persian dagger made of solid gold and decorated with carved lion heads bespeaks the opulence of Xerxes' Empire. The blade was already broken when the dagger was found in the ruins of the ancient Persian city of Ecbatana.

Then, suddenly, they heard the Greeks' battle hymn—"O Saving Lord"—sounding over the water, and saw the first rank of the Greek fleet plunging toward them around the curve of the straits.

The Greek playwright Aeschylus, who fought in the battle, later dramatized the Persian sailors' feelings as their "expectations faded away."

> *This sacred battle-hymn*
> *Did not betoken flight, but stubborn courage*
> *Impetuous for attack. A trumpet sounded,*
> *And at that note their men were fired to action—*
> *With measured beat the oars fell all together,*
> *Sweeping the foam back at the one command,*
> *And soon they all were clearly visible.*
> *First their right wing, advancing in close order*
> *And well-aligned, led on; next the main fleet*
> *Stood out against us.*

The Persians, who had thought to trap the enemy inside the straits, were instead blundering into their own trap.

The two fleets came at each other on a converging course just inside the narrow passage off Aghios Giorgios Island, east of Salamis (*map, page 57*). On the Greeks' right was the commander in chief, Eurybiades, with the contingents from the Peloponnesus. The whole center and left were occupied by the Athenians—200 galleys under Themistocles, filled with men hot to liberate their city and their people. A light south wind played over the straits, fanning the backs of the citizen-rowers as they thrust their ships over the smooth sea.

On the Persian right, the Phoenicians were pushing ahead of the center in their fast, high-decked galleys. On the left rowed the Persians' Ionian confederates, while in the center went a heterogeneous mass of Cypriotes and other Levantine peoples, squadron by squadron, chanting their war songs. The Persians streamed through the channel where it bent west in a jagged curve. And in these narrowing waters their ships jostled, congested and began to lose formation.

The Greeks hit them as they were emerging from the most confined part of the straits, only half a mile wide, giving room for little more than 20 galleys to row abreast. The Athenian line crunched into the advancing Phoenicians, enveloping them in a noose of bronze. The usually fast Phoenician ships, unable to deploy, were crushed, one behind another, between the Greeks and the mainland. At the same time, on the Greek right, the galleys from the Peloponnesus and the nearby city-state of Aegina smashed their prows into the flank of the Ionians before the Persian mass could extend its front into the widening channel.

On one side, the island of Salamis was filled with Greek women and children. On the other, at the foot of Mount Aigaleos on the mainland, seated on a golden throne and surrounded by nervous staff officers and obsequious secretaries, Xerxes watched the battle with mounting fury.

Below him, spread like a model on a glassy sea, raged the conflict that could dissolve his visions of European empire. Instead of fighting an open-sea battle in which numbers would decide the outcome, his ships were being picked off in segments as they filed out of the narrow pass

Divine support for the Greek cause

As the awesome Persian juggernaut bore down on them in 480 B.C., the Greeks placed their faith not only in such leaders as Themistocles *(above)* but also in the divinities thought to control all mortal affairs. One surviving proof of this belief is a chiseled stone slab *(far right)* found in 1959 in the Greek town of Troezen. On it is recorded Themistocles' plan for the defense of Athens—by evacuating the city and defeating its attackers at sea. As significant as the plan's logistics is the resolution "to entrust the city to Athena the Mistress and to all the other gods to guard and defend from the barbarian for the sake of the land."

When the historian Herodotus wrote an account of the Battle of Salamis, he spelled out how this pious hope was answered. According to his chronicle, three divine figures worked in the Greek cause. Poseidon *(center)*, god of the sea, destroyed many of the Persian ships in a storm before the battle began. Zeus *(far right)* played a reluctant role; he did not decide to favor the Greek defenders until they took to their ships. This last-minute decision was prompted by the appeals of his daughter Athena *(near right)*, the protector of Athens—whose participation was unstinting. Many sailors swore that she appeared in the skies to encourage the Greek fleet.

After the battle, says Herodotus, Themistocles gave credit where he believed credit due. He reminded his comrades that "it is not we who have won this victory, but the gods."

A stone slab uncovered in the town of Troezen, located about 40 miles south of Athens, memorializes Themistocles' bold plan for dealing with the Persians.

into the strait. The weight of numbers he had counted on was now in favor of the Greeks, who were thrusting their entire force against the emerging units of the Persian vanguard.

The Athenian and Aeginetan ships had been the first to strike. Lycomedes of Athens sheared away the figurehead of the Phoenician galley opposing him. The Athenian captain Ameinias sent his galley straight for the huge Phoenician flagship, became locked with it, beak to beak, and precipitated a general action as other Greek ships drove to his aid. Then Ariabignes, the admiral leading the Phoenicians—a "brave man," wrote Plutarch, and "by far the strongest and most just of the King's brothers"—led a boarding party over the side. But the Greeks met it and threw the Persians back, pitching the admiral dead into the sea.

As each Persian war galley emerged from the narrow passageway, it was attacked by a Greek vessel. And what had been a disciplined line of assault was now a melee. Dully gleaming rams crashed into hulls, bringing galleys to a shuddering halt and splintering their rows of oars, while marines hacked at one another from the bows and storms of arrows burst around the bulwarks. Sometimes a galley drove deeper into a group of enemy ships and faced a tempest of missiles from either side.

Soon the bronze-clad Greeks began to gain the upper hand. Behind their heavy shields they charged the Persians in organized ranks, pushing inexorably across the bloodstained decks. Persian archers fired desperately at the plumed and metallic robots, but the Greeks continued to hack a path through the thinly armored enemy.

As morning wore on, the light south wind sharpened. A choppy swell, running through the straits, increased the Persians' disorder. The high-decked Phoenician ships rolled and fell afoul of one another, shearing away whole banks of oars and gashing one another's bulwarks with their prows. The low Athenian galleys, striking at them from less confined waters, still held their orderly crescent.

Finally, the Phoenicians broke. The first line, backing out of the combat, clashed with fresher ships pushing up behind it and threw the whole wing into chaos. On the Persian left, the Greek confederates of Xerxes were locked in battle with the Peloponnesians; their contest was hard and equal. But the collapse of the Phoenicians on the Persian right exerted an unbearable pressure on the left as well as the center. One by one the King's squadrons—Cypriote, Cilician, Ionian—began to disintegrate and flee. They had lost not only many fighting shipmates but many of their leaders as well—including Ariabignes, the King's brother, and now Syennesis, the admiral of the Persian center.

The Greeks, realizing that victory was at hand, pressed against the wounded fleet with merciless fury and coordination. While the Athenians fell upon the enemy vessels running for shore, the Aeginetan flotilla mopped up those trying to escape back through the channel. So, wrote Herodotus, "the Persian vessels were no sooner clear of the Athenians than forthwith they fell into the hands of the Aeginetan squadron." Democritus, captain of a galley from the island of Naxos, alone took five Persian ships. And Polycritus of Aegina rammed the Phoenician ship that had captured the heroic Pytheas seven weeks previously.

At this point, Artemisia, Queen of Halicarnassus, tried to extricate her galley from the splintering Persian line. She was well aware that the Athenians, resentful of a woman bearing arms against them, had put a heavy price on her capture. Hemmed in by supporting Persian ships and attacked by Ameinias' trireme, she spun about and rammed the nearest galley in her path. It was one of the Persian ships, and its crewmen were all drowned. But the accident deceived Ameinias, who took the Queen's warship for that of a Greek or a Persian deserter and turned away, permitting her to escape. Xerxes' staff, from their distance on the hilltop, also assumed that the sinking ship was that of an enemy.

"Seest thou, master, how well Artemisia fights?" asked one of them, "and how she has just sunk a ship of the enemy?"

"My men have behaved like women," answered Xerxes sadly, "my women like men."

By now the battle had become a rout, and the Ionians, their spirits broken, were fleeing after the Phoenicians down the channel and into the open sea. The 400 Persian soldiers who had been landed the night before on the island of Psyttaleia were isolated. A force of Athenians promptly sailed across from Salamis and massacred them.

The straits had become a theater of horror. Half-sunken hulks drifted like ghost ships among a flotsam of corpses and broken spars. The victorious Greeks, moving through the floating detritus, found Persian sailors and marines clinging to the remains of their ships in the warm water. Without bothering to expend arrows on them, they split open their heads with pieces of wreckage or with their oars. Thousands more in the Persian fleet, unable to swim, had drowned as their ships capsized. Broken galleys covered the shore, and a strong west wind carried many others out into the Aegean, scattering the wreckage with its pitiful human debris along the coasts and reefs beyond Phaleron.

The killing lasted until midnight. At least 200 Persian galleys were sunk, and very likely a great many more had been captured, to be added to the Greek fleet, which had lost only 40 ships.

The Battle of Salamis dealt a crushing blow to Xerxes' hopes. Though the Persian army would fight for another year before giving up the cause, Xerxes, cut off from his homeland, had good reason to fear that his Empire might split asunder. Within a few days of the battle, he and his fleet turned toward Asia. So demoralized were some of Xerxes' sailors that, as they made for the Hellespont, they mistook some low rocks for Greek galleys lying in wait for them, and fled in panic to the open sea.

If Salamis had not been won—if the Persians had conquered—the whole stream of Western history must have changed its bed. For within a century the tiny states of Greece, by esthetic and intellectual passion, had laid the foundation of the modern era. Just as the Parthenon, completed within 42 years of Salamis, held in its marble proportions the harmony and mathematic rigor of Greece in its prime, so the great Greek thinkers—Socrates, Plato, Aristotle—established the philosophic discipline of the future Western world. In art, in science, in literature, these few peoples, in their fleeting heyday, created the first known civilization in which reason predominated over religious faith or superstition.

That future civilization, with its 2,500-year-old legacy of free imagination and rational thought, was won by the ships and men of Salamis.

The lethal evolution of galleys

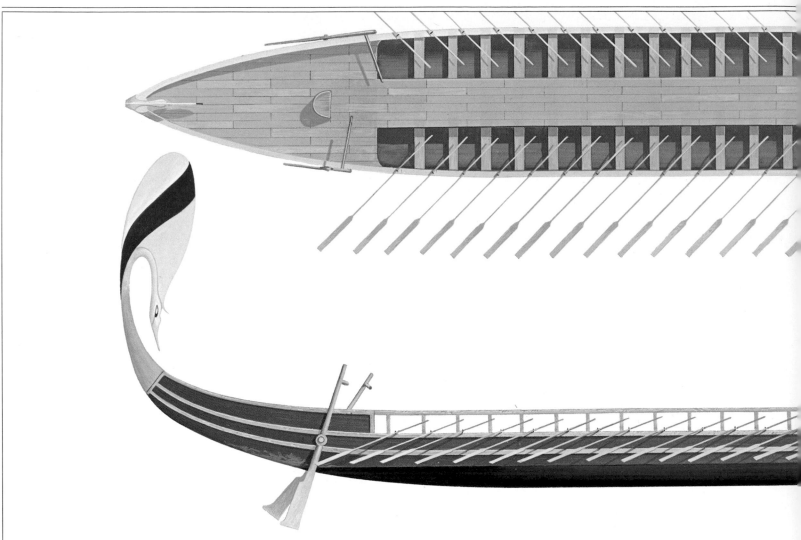

Generating thrust for ramming

From the dawn of seagoing warfare, fighting ships depended mainly on oars for propulsion. Egyptians had oared warships as early as 1600 B.C., and the Achaeans about 400 years later used galleys rowed by 20 or more men. The advent of the ram placed a premium on power, and by the Sixth Century B.C. most eastern Mediterranean navies had long, sleek ramming craft—monoremes—driven by 50 oars (above).

Lengthening ships to accommodate oarsmen, however, exacted a price in maneuverability. Some inspired Phoenician or Greek shipwright took another approach—placing the oarsmen on two levels. The success of the new two-banked warship, a bireme, inevitably led to the trireme (pages 70-71), a three-banked craft that was the best compromise between power and manageability.

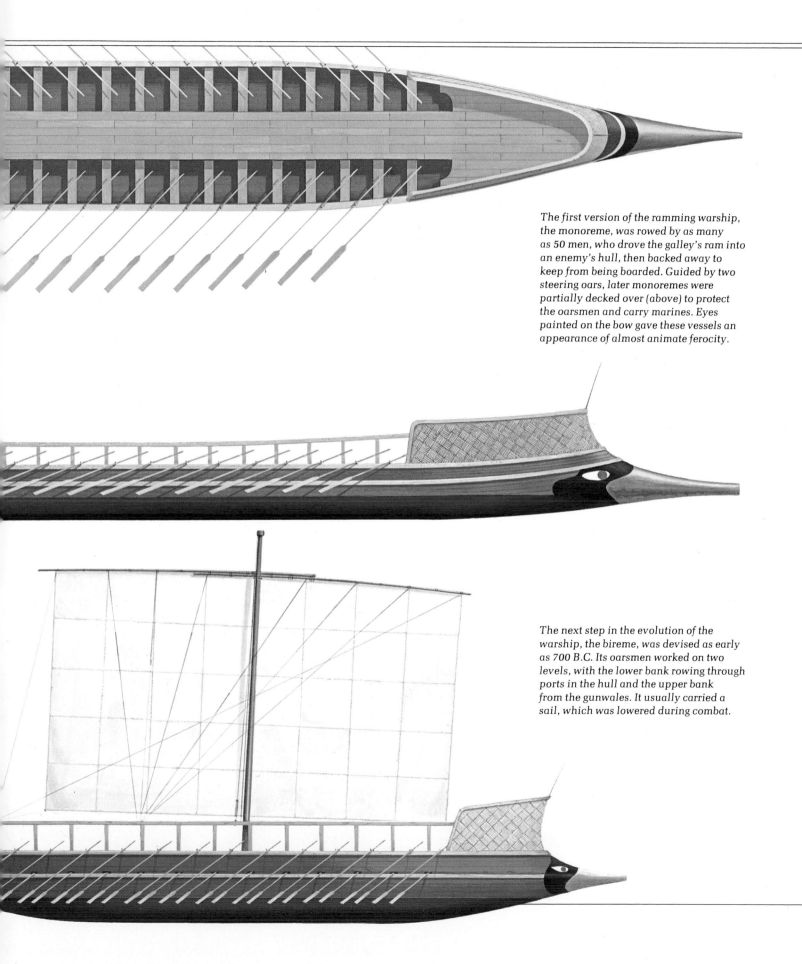

The first version of the ramming warship, the monoreme, was rowed by as many as 50 men, who drove the galley's ram into an enemy's hull, then backed away to keep from being boarded. Guided by two steering oars, later monoremes were partially decked over (above) to protect the oarsmen and carry marines. Eyes painted on the bow gave these vessels an appearance of almost animate ferocity.

The next step in the evolution of the warship, the bireme, was devised as early as 700 B.C. Its oarsmen worked on two levels, with the lower bank rowing through ports in the hull and the upper bank from the gunwales. It usually carried a sail, which was lowered during combat.

Triple-tiered ship of the line

Early in the Sixth Century B.C., apparently in the Greek city-state of Corinth, naval architects found a way to fit a third bank of oarsmen into a galley: They added an outrigger to the hull *(right)*, producing the trireme, the most effective warship of the ancient world. The classic Greek trireme became a 120-foot-long waterborne juggernaut with a multi-pronged ram; it was about 12 feet wide, flaring to 16 feet at the outrigger gunwale that held its top bank of oarsmen.

With a complement of up to 170 oarsmen, the nimble, shallow-draft galley could puncture an enemy's hull with tremendous force, then reverse its thrust to pull free in a trice. Triremes were the ships of the line at the Battle of Salamis in 480 B.C. And despite efforts to build larger craft *(page 72)*, the trireme—given new names as more men were added to the three banks of oars—remained the workhorse of every navy in the Mediterranean for seven centuries.

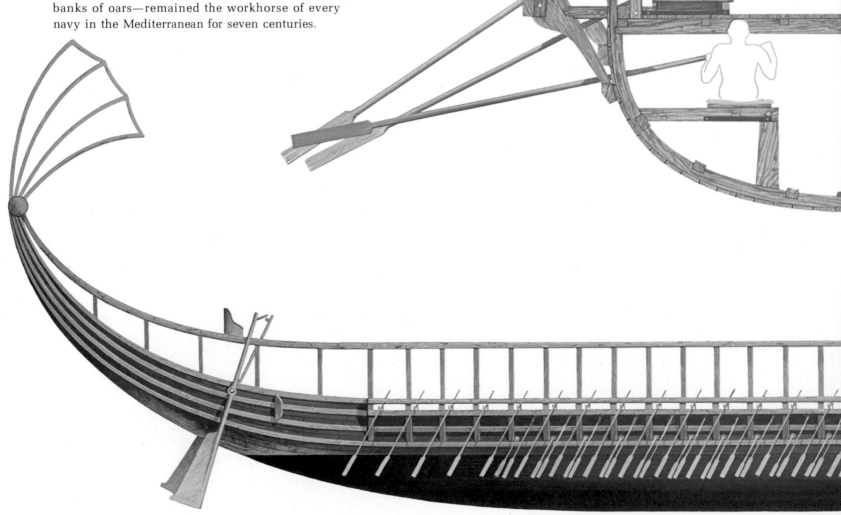

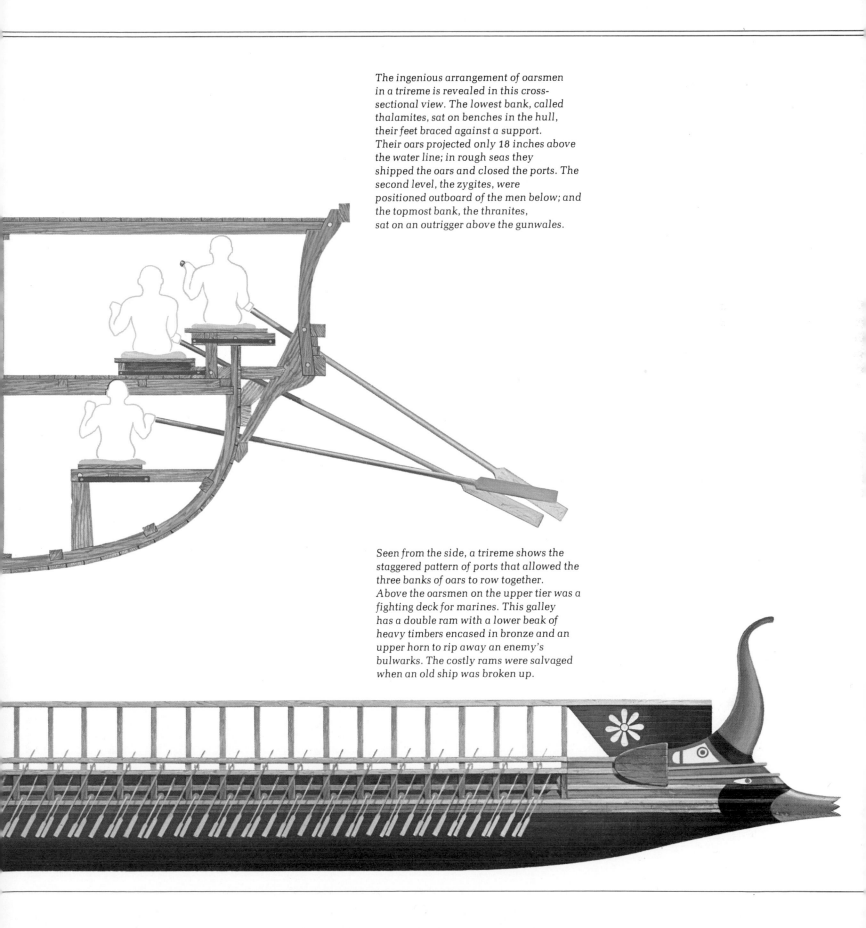

The ingenious arrangement of oarsmen in a trireme is revealed in this cross-sectional view. The lowest bank, called thalamites, sat on benches in the hull, their feet braced against a support. Their oars projected only 18 inches above the water line; in rough seas they shipped the oars and closed the ports. The second level, the zygites, were positioned outboard of the men below; and the topmost bank, the thranites, sat on an outrigger above the gunwales.

Seen from the side, a trireme shows the staggered pattern of ports that allowed the three banks of oars to row together. Above the oarsmen on the upper tier was a fighting deck for marines. This galley has a double ram with a lower beak of heavy timbers encased in bronze and an upper horn to rip away an enemy's bulwarks. The costly rams were salvaged when an old ship was broken up.

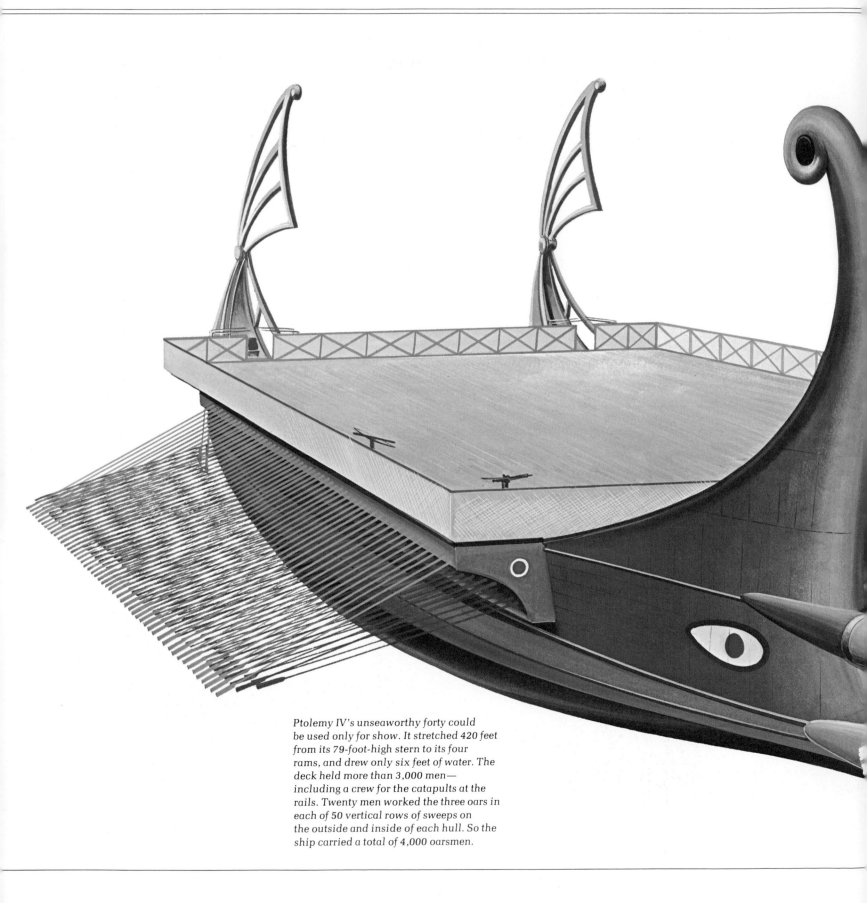

Ptolemy IV's unseaworthy forty could
be used only for show. It stretched 420 feet
from its 79-foot-high stern to its four
rams, and drew only six feet of water. The
deck held more than 3,000 men—
including a crew for the catapults at the
rails. Twenty men worked the three oars in
each of 50 vertical rows of sweeps on
the outside and inside of each hull. So the
ship carried a total of 4,000 oarsmen.

Probing the limits of oar power

Shipwrights tried to enlarge on the classic trireme, but soon found they had achieved the ultimate number of banks of oarsmen: A taller ship became unseaworthy. However, hulls could be longer and wider, and men could be added to each oar. Thus were born the polyremes—fivers, seveners, tenners, and up.

These terms designated the number of men on each set of oars in a vertical line from the top to bottom banks: A fiver might have two men at the top oar, two on the middle and one on the bottom.

In the Third Century B.C., Ptolemy IV of Egypt built a twin-hulled forty *(left)*, which proved too clumsy for battle. By the First Century B.C., builders realized they had exceeded the efficient size for a warship, and the trireme, with more men at each oar, became the basic war galley for three more centuries.

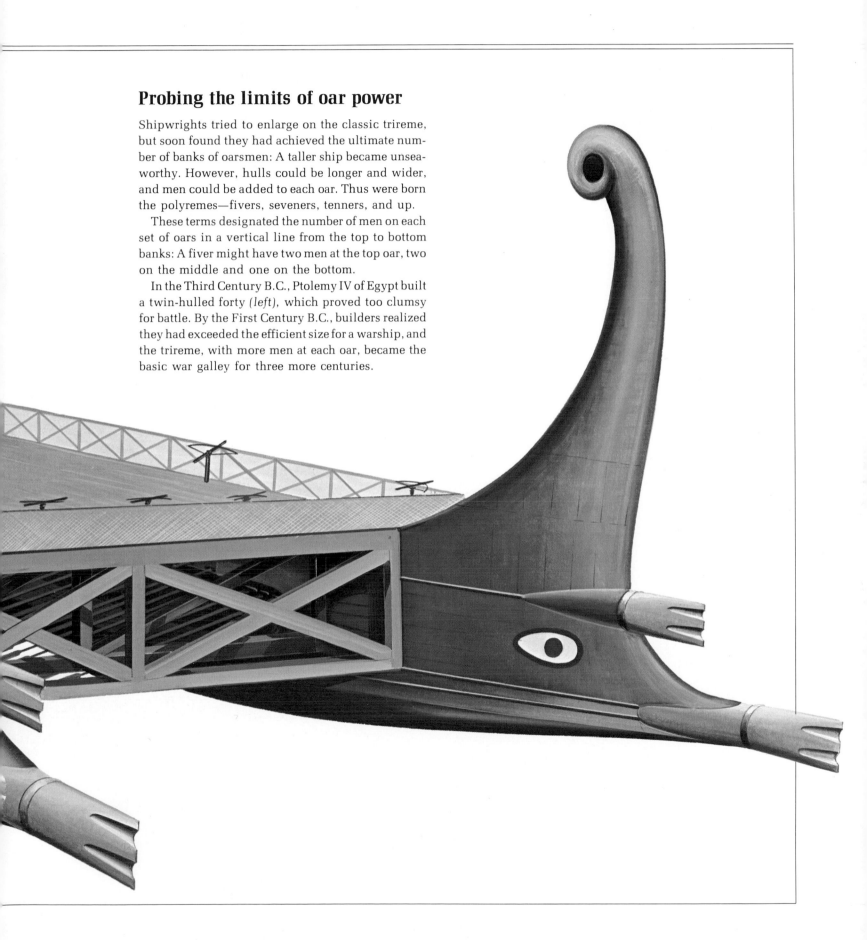

Chapter 3

An efflorescence of trade

thens' golden age was born in the convulsion of the Battle of Salamis. For the Athenians, the prize of victory was a progressive democratization of their government and society; and that, in turn, helped produce an explosion of artistic and intellectual accomplishment. Along with cultural progress came a prodigious expansion of commerce, most of it inevitably conducted by sea.

There were few roads in Greece, and from earliest times Greek traders had turned their gaze seaward. "Cross-channel men" they were called as they sailed from island to island on the shimmering Aegean, a benign sea that for more than half the year offered voyagers steady winds and rarely imperiled them with storms. Nor had Greek mariners hesitated to reach out for more distant markets. By 1200 B.C., for example, their vessels were riding the trade winds south to the Nile; 600 years later the Egyptians authorized the founding of the Greek merchant town of Naucratis, 10 miles from the great river and linked to it by a newly dug canal. From Naucratis' four warehouses, the settlers sent home precious cargoes of linen and papyrus.

Like various other city-states, Athens had at first been largely self-sufficient, its moderate wants supplied by its native craftsmen and farmers. But by the beginning of the Sixth Century B.C., the population was growing more rapidly than the local grain supply. A statesman named Solon responded to the situation by banning the sale to foreign markets of all agricultural products except the city-state's fine olives and oil. These were shipped abroad to pay for urgently needed imports, primarily grain from the Nile Valley and the northern shores of the Black Sea. An assortment of luxuries were imported as well. From the Persian Gulf and the great Phoenician entrepôts of Tyre and Carthage traveled ivory, frankincense, carpets and a coveted purple dye extracted from a shellfish, the *purpura murex.*

Maritime vigor did more than provide the city-state with sustenance and exotica; it also promised to earn Athens position and influence in the Mediterranean world. This was expressed as a rhetorical question by the political leader who became the embodiment of Athens in the era after Salamis, an aristocratic democrat named Pericles: "How can mere farmers, with no knowledge of the sea, achieve anything worthy of note?" A seagoing people—he might have added—need acknowledge no limits.

Ironically, given Pericles' sentiment, the owners of many of Athens' merchant vessels were not Athenians. A number of foreigners—from Syria, Syracuse, Ionia—took up permanent residence in Athens. Since they did not hold citizenship, they were barred by law from owning land, but there was nothing in the city's statutes to prevent them from investing in shipping. It thus became commonplace for an alien of means to purchase a ship and a slave crew, then charter out the vessel, with himself as skipper.

The merchant who chartered the ship from this owner-captain typically did so with borrowed money. Along the quayside of Athens' port of Piraeus, there was no shortage of investors willing to supply the funds the merchant needed to purchase a cargo and pay the charter fee. The

On a cup dating from the Sixth Century B.C., the King of Cyrene—a Greek colony on the north coast of Africa— supervises the weighing, packing and storing of silphium, a plant thought to have beneficial medical properties.

investors were plentifully rewarded: They received interest ranging as high as 30 per cent for the few months that their money was tied up in such ventures. The merchants were content to pay these rates because they could reasonably expect to sell the cargo abroad for twice the amount of the loan.

The owner-captain generally loaded the merchant's goods and set out in spring, as soon as the winter storms had subsided. His round-hulled vessel resembled a clumsy mongrel when it sailed alongside the sleek triremes patrolling the seaways of the Aegean. Built for capacity and seaworthiness rather than for speed or maneuverability, it had a deep, high-sided hull that could carry 100 to 150 tons; some larger merchant ships could accommodate as much as 400 tons. Such vessels were driven by a single broad mainsail. With a brisk following wind they could plod along at four knots; when tacking clumsily against head winds, they slowed to half that speed.

If the owner-captain was in the coastal trade, he would lay his course along the shore, perhaps traveling westward to the Italian ports of Syracuse, Rhegium and Neapolis, or traveling southeast past Asia Minor to Byblos, Sidon and Tyre in Syria. (Many coast-hugging vessels were small enough to run up onto the tideless beach at night, putting out to sea again in the morning.) If bound for Naucratis in Egypt or Cyrene in Libya, the captain would strike out across the Mediterranean, depending on the stars, occasional landmarks, and the feel of the wind to guide him to his destination.

The unhurried course of the usual voyage to the principal Mediterranean ports meant that merchant vessels could complete only one round trip a year. By September or early October, the ships would come lumbering back into Piraeus. The merchants would count up their profits, if any, and pay off their investors. The shipowners would pocket their charter fees and haul their vessels onto the beach for the winter. Sometimes, however, a merchant and his investors would wait in vain for sight of the ship. She might have been delayed and hauled up in another port until the next sailing season—or her owner-captain might be in the hands of pirates.

Piracy had subsided since the chaotic era of the Sea Peoples at the end of the Second Millenium B.C., but it never ceased altogether; the rich cargoes of trading vessels were simply too tempting. Usually the corsairs would dispose of their booty in the nearest port, but they were sometimes willing to let the ship and its owner go free in return for a suitably large cash payment. The merchants and their backers could be counted on to help pay the ransom—providing it was less than what a total loss would amount to.

Piracy was not the only danger confronting the Greeks; despite Athens' victory at Salamis, there remained a threat from the Persian Empire. During the winter of 478-477 B.C., Athenians broached the idea of a league of Greek city-states to defend one another against any new attacks from Xerxes' forces. The league's members—numbering between 250 and 300 when the alliance was at its zenith—included not only the city-states on the mainland, but also some in Asia Minor, on the many Aegean islands, on the Sea of Marmara and in Thrace. All

A lacework of sea-lanes

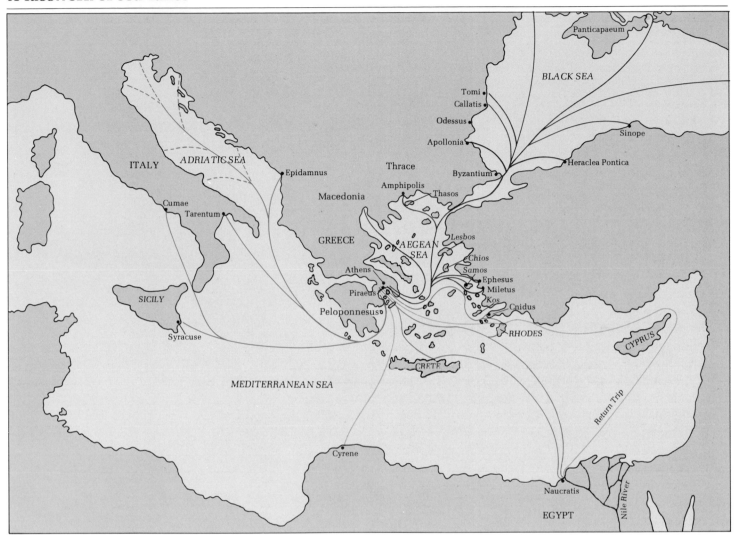

In its golden age, Greece spread
tentacles of trade in all directions. From
Piraeus, westbound ships sailed to
Italy, Sicily, and the head of the Adriatic.
The all-important grain route went
northeast through the Black Sea. Other
traders voyaged south to Egypt for
exotic goods transshipped from the Orient;
on their return trip, the prevailing
northerlies forced them to travel northeast
and around Cyprus before heading home.

the allies contributed ships, if they were able, or money to keep the
shipyards of Athens occupied. Since the treasury was originally located on the sacred Aegean island of Delos, the alliance became known
as the Delian League.

All members had an equal voice at meetings, but Athens' overwhelm-
ing naval power enabled it to dominate the Delian League and use it as
the foundation of a commercial empire. Athenian weights and measures
became the standard units for transactions, and Athens' distinctive coinage, engraved with an owl, became as omnipresent in the Mediterranean as the olive oil that the city-state sent forth in the fired clay
pots called amphorae.

Soon Piraeus had vaulted to a position of ascendancy among the ports
of the eastern Mediterranean. Through a narrow entrance formed by
two stone moles that reached out to enclose the harbor, a steady stream
of vessels came and went. Many of the incoming ships carried grain from
the Black Sea. If pirates were menacing the trade routes that season,
some of these vital grain fleets would sail in convoys, with triremes

spider-legging alongside them. The warships not only protected the grain ships from corsairs but sometimes towed them through calms or against unfavorable winds.

As a convoy approached Piraeus the triremes would speed on ahead, some peeling off to go into two adjacent bays that served primarily as naval stations. The others, passing through the gateway to the port, would turn to the right side of the harbor, which was also reserved for the navy. At all three of these naval bases the sleek, thin-skinned warships were hauled out and stored in long sheds (pages 46-47) on the shore. The trireme periodically needed drying out to keep its fragile hull from becoming waterlogged.

If the breeze was dying as the grain ships neared their destination, rowboats would come out to cluster around them, taking their bowlines and towing them into port. Within the harbor there was so little room to maneuver that ships were pulled to their moorings even if they had sailed through the entrance on their own. Meanwhile, customs inspectors boarded the vessels to collect the standard 2 per cent levy on all cargo entering or leaving Piraeus. Port agents also charged fees for the use of the harbor facilities.

The heart of Piraeus was a single long quay alive with activity. A newly arrived vessel would be tied to the quay bow on, and a gangplank would be laid across to the pier or, if its goods were being transshipped, to another vessel rafted alongside. Behind the forest of gently rocking masts stood half a dozen huge warehouses, with lines of porters filing like ants in and out of their wide, columned entrances. Largest of all these structures was the Long Colonnade, a cornucopia of grain. By law, Athenian traders were required to bring all grain cargoes home to Piraeus. Only a third of this grain could then be transshipped abroad; the rest was apportioned to wholesalers—in small lots, to make sure that no one dealer could corner the market.

Beneath the porticoes of the Long Colonnade, grain dealers called out the latest prices amid clouds of dust and chaff. Within the adjacent colonnades, other merchants hawked salt fish from the Black Sea, cheese from Sicily, incense from Arabia, figs from Asia Minor, salt pork from Italy, and timber from Macedonia. There was also an active market for a living commodity: slaves. These might be prisoners of war or hapless souls who had been purchased from pirates or barbarian chiefs; and any child of a slave was automatically enslaved and thus subject to sale as well.

The slaves of Athens numbered nearly a third of the city's population. The less fortunate among them performed such grueling manual labor as digging silver in the nearby mines. Luckier members of this under class served as domestics in wealthy households or as clerks or crewmen on ships. Often the more fortunate slaves worked their way up to positions of responsibility; slave sailors might even rise to captain's rank. A number of enterprising slaves made themselves so indispensable to their masters that they were eventually awarded their freedom. A man named Pasion, jointly owned by a pair of Athenian bankers, started as a porter, turned to accounting, advanced to become the head of a bank, then branched out into shipowning and the manufacture of shields. He

Pericles, the leader of Athens from 460 to 429 B.C., guided the city-state to its zenith in art and commerce. He directed the building of the Parthenon and other temples and saw that Athens had a strong navy to protect its merchant marine.

not only earned his freedom but was granted Athenian citizenship as well—a rare attainment.

In the slave market and all along the teeming Piraeus quayside, the chorus of commercial activity continued through the length of the day and well into the night under summer skies—until the cooling winds of September signaled an end to the sailing season. By midautumn, the ranks of wholesalers, middlemen and money-changers had retreated from the waterfront. The shutters were closed on the long warehouses. And by December the only reminder of the hectic summer circus at Piraeus was the sound of wooden hulls creaking alongside the wharves, where they waited out the winter for the resumption of the shipping season in April.

Year after year, this annual ebbing and flowing of commerce grew in strength. "The wares of the whole world find their way to us," Pericles boasted; and in his role as the most influential member of the city-state's governing board of seven generals, he encouraged a program of peaceful commercial expansion over one based on conquest. Nevertheless, the might of Athens stirred the fears of many neighboring governments, including two Peloponnesian city-states, Corinth and Sparta. The Corinthians succeeded in persuading the proudly self-reliant Spartans that unless they took military action against Athens they would surrender all semblance of independence. The result of their cajoling was the outbreak of the Peloponnesian War in 431 B.C. Except for one brief interval of peace, the conflict would last for 27 years—and end with the complete defeat of Athens.

Throughout the long War the Athenians invested their faith and energy in naval supremacy and carefully avoided being drawn into land combat. They went so far as to permit Sparta's plainly superior army—30,000 regulars plus reserves, twice the size of their own land force—to invade the countryside of Attica, the peninsular setting of Athens. The villagers who lived there were evacuated to the city, where they found safety behind the so-called Long Walls, an effective series of fortifications that surrounded the metropolis and extended along both sides of a road to Piraeus, enclosing the port as well. There, a constant procession of cargo vessels continued to unload food and other necessities for those within the barricades.

The Long Walls proved impregnable, but the terrible overcrowding behind them had a fatal consequence. A plague, possibly typhus, erupted in Athens and took the lives of a quarter of the population, including Pericles. After his death in 429, his successors fought among themselves over what policy to follow—whether to end the War through negotiation or to continue it in more aggressive fashion. Neither the peace party nor the war party was able to assume undisputed command, and the Peloponnesian War dragged on until a series of defeats compelled the Athenians to sign a peace treaty in 421. Three years later, however, a new Athenian leader, Alcibiades, convinced the citizens to resume warfare. Athenian naval power enabled them to carry on the fight for another 13 years. Then the struggle ended suddenly, almost anticlimactically—and at sea.

Athens' navy was by this time down to 180 triremes, three fifths of her

A tidy trader's last voyage

Hunting for shipwrecks near Kyrenia on the north coast of Cyprus in 1967, underwater archeologists from the University of Pennsylvania Museum were led by a Cypriote diver to a small heap of amphorae 100 feet down on the sea bottom. Beneath the jars was an extraordinary find—the well-preserved skeleton of a Greek trading vessel that sank 23 centuries ago. From the remains of the hull, scholars have surmised many details of her construction, permitting this artist's rendition of the vessel's skipper supervising the loading before her last voyage.

The Kyrenian ship's 14½-foot beam and 47-foot length provided excellent cargo space. A single sail —700 square feet of linen bent on a 40-foot yard— gave her a top speed of about five knots; brailing lines attached to the yard could alter the shape and angle of the sail to make the best use of the winds. When fully loaded with seven tons of cargo, she had only two feet of freeboard; however, woven matting along her gunwales protected cargo stored on deck.

Bronze coins found among the timbers show that the vessel sank no earlier than 306 B.C., and carbon dating indicates that she had been built 80 years earlier. The decades took their toll: There is evidence of major repairs. But, to the end, she voyaged widely, as proved by her last cargo: 404 amphorae, mostly from Rhodes; 29 millstones from the Aegean island of Kos; and the shells of 10,000 almonds, probably picked up on Cyprus shortly before she went to the bottom.

The restored hull of the Kyrenian vessel lies in a museum not far from the spot where she foundered. Her discoverers, knowing that the ancient timbers would disintegrate when exposed to air, soaked each piece of the hull in fresh water as it was brought up, and then immersed it in polyethylene glycol, a waxlike chemical that helped restore the bulk and strength of the wood.

force at the beginning of the War. To guard the vital grain shipments from Russia, the triremes were sent, in 405 B.C., to the Hellespont, the narrow strait leading from the Aegean to the Sea of Marmara and thence to the Black Sea. Each day the rowers and fighting men beached their crowded vessels and went ashore to eat and sleep. Meanwhile, a large Spartan naval force stealthily followed. After five days, Spartan scouts signaled that most of the Athenian warships were drawn up along the barren shore and that their crews had gone inland to the nearest town for food. The main Spartan fleet swept down on the undefended vessels. Only nine triremes, under the command of a quick-thinking Athenian named Conon, managed to escape the assault, raising their sails to a brisk northeasterly wind and fleeing from the Spartan triremes, whose sails had been left ashore.

At one blow the Athenian sea dynasty had come to an end. Sparta took steps to ensure that Athens would not fight again. To the doleful music of flute players, the defeated people and their conquerors tore down the Long Walls that had sheltered the city and its port for so many years. And the Athenians were forced to accept the presence of a Spartan garrison in their city.

Even this humiliating outcome could not entirely dim the glory of Athens. The experienced traders of Piraeus were able to hold their elaborate overseas network together; they had both incentive and encouragement to do so, since Athens remained dependent on distant markets for the necessities of life. But much else would change in the years to come, not just for Athens but for all of Greece. During the following century, two invaders from the north, father and son, would overthrow the old order and bring a forcibly united Greece to a new and quite different golden age.

In 359 B.C. a resourceful and ambitious warrior, Philip II, became ruler of the sprawling kingdom of Macedonia, north of the Greek peninsula. Philip looked enviously on the territories to the south—particularly Athens, which he recognized as the ultimate in refined civilization (and whose citizens regarded him and his Macedonians as semibarbarians). To capture this jewel and the rest of Greece, Philip created an armed force of deadly efficiency. Its infantrymen were rigorously trained to fight in a new formation known as the phalanx. Each phalanx consisted of 256 men arrayed in a square; the 16 men in each of the first five ranks would extend their 14-foot spears straight ahead, while those in the next 11 ranks would rest theirs on the shoulders of the men in front of them, creating a dense and terrifying grove of weaponry. Such sections could be deployed individually or joined to form a giant phalanx of several thousand infantrymen, an intimidating body that brushed aside opposition and cleared the way for cavalry charges to wipe up any remnants of resistance.

With this formidable instrument to back up his threats, Philip was able to play off the squabbling politicians of the Greek city-states against one another, enlarging his dominion by strong-arm diplomacy. On a number of occasions he contracted marriages to cement an alliance; he had six or seven wives in all. And when necessary, he resorted to force—as he

A monetary mélange

As maritime commerce expanded through the Mediterranean in the Fifth Century B.C., barter, which had served the farmer and city dweller as a means of trade since earliest times, was largely supplanted by the use of money. In Athens' trading center, the harbor of Piraeus, a focus of activity was a row of tables where money-changers called out the latest exchange rates for the various currencies shippers brought into port.

Coins of many realms were accepted at first. But as more and more foreign merchants did business there and the complications of international trade increased, the money-changers gradually established a preference for a few trustworthy currencies—including the three at right.

Gold, always valuable, was the metal of coinage brought from the eastern Mediterranean states ruled by Persia. Greece had little gold but ample silver; so the Greek city-states opted for silver coinage, each city-state issuing its own. Silver coinage from Cyzicus, the Greek city-state and trading mecca at the entrance to the Black Sea, was a prominent currency.

But when Athens came to dominate the confederation of Greek states known as the Delian League, Athenian merchants not only forced the transfer of the league's treasury from the island of Delos to their home city, but also pressured the other members into adopting their currency. Soon Athenian coinage (right center) was the most widely exchanged in the eastern Mediterranean.

Three widely accepted currencies of Fifth and Fourth Century Mediterranean commerce were the gold daric of Persia (top), embellished with a spear-carrying archer; the owl-decorated silver coin of Athens (center); and a silver coin from the city-state of Cyzicus, featuring the infant Hercules subduing snakes.

had to in order to subdue Athens. By 338 B.C. virtually all Greece was in the Macedonian's grasp.

After consolidating his control of Greece, Philip began laying plans for military adventures farther afield: He had determined to march eastward and conquer the Persian Empire, which at the time stretched all the way from Asia Minor to the borders of India. But in 336 B.C., before he could embark on this grand undertaking, he was assassinated, perhaps by a Persian agent or an agent of Philip's first wife, who was jealous of one of the younger women he had married. Philip was succeeded on the throne by his son Alexander, just 20 years old—and so palpably ambitious that it was said by some that he was the one who had hired his father's killer.

Alexander shared his father's designs on the Persian Empire, and he was an even more brilliant general. Like his Greek subjects, he visualized the world as a cluster of three continents—Europe, Africa and Asia—surrounded by a single, embracing ocean. In 334 B.C., at the age of 22, he set out to conquer this world. Because he also intended to forge new sea routes to link Asia with Africa and Europe, he saw to it that his army included shipwrights and sailors to form a makeshift navy that would be used for explorations of the watery southern reaches of the then-known world.

From the beginning, there was no stopping him. Intrepid and headstrong, Alexander made decisions swiftly, took extraordinary risks, delighted in personal combat and manipulated his 35,000-man army with dazzling panache. Marching east, he first drove the Persians out of Asia Minor and the Levant. Then he swept south to Egypt, conquering every army in his path. Turning eastward again, he led his army through Persia and on toward India, reaching the banks of the Indus River in 326 B.C. There, his shipwrights constructed galleys to ferry his troops across.

Then the subcontinent swallowed the invader. There seemed no end to this hostile country, with its monsoon-swollen rivers and stubborn enemies who fought from the backs of monstrous elephants that panicked his horses. It took nearly a year to push 250 miles beyond the Indus; by then, Alexander's men had been on the march eastward for nearly eight years and had traversed approximately 8,000 miles. Finally, they refused to go farther.

Near Nicaea on the Hydaspes River—a tributary of the Indus—Alexander put his shipwrights to work creating a fleet of 1,800 transports and galleys. Once completed, the fleet set off downriver toward the Indian Ocean, with the bulk of the army marching along the banks. For nine months the combined force moved along the 800-mile passage to the Indus delta. In the late summer of 325 B.C., Alexander sailed into the open sea and poured a libation to the gods of the deep, flinging the golden cup into the waves.

The time had come for the conqueror to consolidate his gains and establish a nautical link between the eastern and western reaches of his new empire. Alexander entrusted the job of forging this link to a seawise Cretan named Nearchus. Some of the 1,800 vessels had been lost on the way down the Indus; the exact number is unrecorded. But Nearchus took command of the remaining fleet, selecting for his crewmen any soldiers who had experience at sea. His instructions were to find his way west to the mouth of the Tigris River, and then to sail up the river to a rendezvous with Alexander at Susa in Persia.

The seaborne expedition along the northern shore of the Indian Ocean to the Persian Gulf would prove replete with adversities, which the admiral recorded in a journal. His account has been lost, but a Greek historian named Arrian paraphrased it in a narrative composed several centuries later.

Nearchus ran into difficulties while still negotiating the estuary at the mouth of the Indus: The late-summer monsoon blew onshore with such strength that the fleet could not work its way forward. Not until the end of September had the wind eased sufficiently for the ships to reach the river's mouth. There the voyagers suffered another setback. Accustomed to the tideless waters of their own sea, they were astonished by a huge, roaring tidal bore that swept into the estuary from the Indian Ocean, damaging some of their ships and destroying others. Nearchus, after recovering from his surprise, noticed that the retreating tide had uncovered yet another obstacle—an impassable bar at the river mouth, formed by silt deposited over the years by the waters of the Indus. He did not let it detain him for long. Taking a work gang out to the bar at low tide, he directed them to cut a passage through the obstruction; then, at slack high water, Nearchus led his fleet through the newly created channel into the open ocean.

The still-active monsoon continued to slow the fleet, however, and about 20 miles west of the mouth of the Indus, Nearchus was forced to put into a harbor—the site of present-day Karachi. For 24 days he and his men camped on the shore, subsisting on mussels and oysters and standing watch behind hastily built rock fortifications while tribesmen studied them with a malevolent eye.

When the monsoon finally abated at the end of October, Nearchus took his fleet to sea again, staying close to the coast and often passing between the mainland and nearby islands. Some of these passages were mere channels, one so narrow that the galleys' oars struck against rocks on both sides. At other points, shoals and heavy surf forced the fleet out to sea. Fearing to proceed in the dark while negotiating such perilous stretches of coastline, Nearchus anchored his ships at dusk, and the men passed the night huddled in their cramped galleys, retching with seasickness. On those occasions when they were able to beach their galleys, the sailors frequently found the land barren and without fresh water.

The voyagers finally approached a coastal village that held promise of provisions—only to be met at the shore by 600 tribesmen who threatened them with spears. However, Nearchus noticed that the "thick spears of the barbarians were adapted only for close fight, and were by no means formidable as missiles." So he ordered his best swimmers to jump over the side and swim until they found their footing. In the shallows, they were to form a file three deep, then "rush forward shouting the war cry" and shooting their arrows, while the men on the galleys provided covering fire.

The villagers on the shore stood their ground as Nearchus' men swam

This ivory miniature, found with its top missing, is believed to represent the Fourth Century B.C. warrior-king Philip II of Macedonia, conqueror of Greece and father of Alexander the Great.

toward them. But when the Greeks charged, the tribesmen panicked and fled. The sailors captured a few of them. Some were clothed in hides, others in the skins of large fish. They "had shaggy hair, not only on their head, but all over their body," according to Arrian's account. "Their nails resembled the claws of wild beasts, and were used, it would seem, instead of iron for dividing fish and splitting the softer kinds of wood, for iron they had none."

After appropriating the food in the village and making some overdue repairs on his ships, Nearchus proceeded on his way. The journey brought him to other settlements that proved less hostile. One group of villagers welcomed the seagoing strangers, giving them some of their prized sheep; when the sailors expressed puzzlement at the fishy taste of the mutton, their hosts explained that the sheep were fed on fish because their poor land could not provide fodder.

To the Mediterranean men, this bleak coast—a "country with no pastures and hardly even a blade of grass"—was little better than the deserts they had marched through on their way east. Most of the inhabitants subsisted largely on fish, crabs and oysters. The few scattered palm trees were stripped of their bark to make nets that the fishermen spread alongshore at high tide: They had no boats in which to go fishing at sea. Small fish were eaten raw, and the larger ones were left in the sun to dry and be pounded into meal.

Whales were another of the region's few resources. They occasionally ventured too close to shore, were stranded and died. The shore dwellers evidently did not eat whale meat, but when one of the giant carcasses had rotted—and could be approached without suffocation from the stench—they would cut away the whalebone and employ it to build crude huts. Traveling up the coast, Nearchus and his sailors marveled at beams and rafters made from rib bones and doors fashioned from the whales' great jaws.

At sea, Nearchus' fleet encountered some living whales. Nothing like them had been seen in the Mediterranean, and at the first sight of a pod of the huge creatures sending their spouts high in the air, the men in the boats were "greatly alarmed and, through astonishment, let the oars drop from their hands." Nearchus urged them forward. Shouting, splashing their oars and blowing their trumpets, the Greeks charged at the whales, which prudently sounded beneath them, surfacing at a safe distance to spout again.

In the best Homeric tradition, Nearchus' odyssey even included a supposedly enchanted island, located near the mouth of the Kalami River on the coast of present-day Pakistan. When one of the fleet's transports disappeared while traversing the area, a local pilot recruited by Nearchus explained that the island was the domain of a supernatural being who would seduce any sailor landing on the shore and then transform him into a fish. Nearchus sent one of his 30-oared galleys around the island in search of the lost transport. The sailors called out the names of their missing shipmates, but their shouts were met by silence. Seeing no alternative but to test the truth of the legend, the intrepid Nearchus led his men ashore—without ill effects. Still, the fate of the transport and its crew remained a mystery. Presumably, the lost vessel had blun-

One of the finest sculpted images of Alexander was discovered at Tarsus, in present-day Turkey. The marble figure was evidently carved long after the death of Alexander in Persia in 323 B.C.

dered onto one of the rocky shoals surrounding the island. Arrian, summing up the incident in the severe tones of the historian, commented, "Now, for my part I have no praise to bestow on Nearchus for expending so much time and ingenuity on the not very difficult task of proving the falsehood of these stories, for to take up antiquated fables merely with a view to prove their falsehood, I can only regard as a contemptible piece of folly."

In December of 325 B.C. the weary, sunburned sailors finally reached the Gulf of Oman and turned northwest into the Persian Gulf. Here they found abundant food and fresh water. Some of the sailors went exploring a few miles inland where, as Arrian reports, they "fell in with a man who wore a Greek mantle, and was otherwise attired as a Greek and spoke the Greek language. Those who first discovered him declared that tears started to their eyes, so strange did it appear, after all they had suffered, to see once more a countryman of their own, and to hear the accents of their native tongue." The man explained that he was a straggler from Alexander's army and that the King "was not more than a five days' march distant from the sea."

At this, Nearchus, an aide and five of his sailors set off to bring their commander the good news that his fleet was still intact. By the time they reached the royal headquarters, the travelers were more bedraggled than ever—"their hair long and neglected, their persons filthy, encrusted all over with brine and shriveled, their complexion sallow from want of sleep and other severe privations. It was not without difficulty that Alexander, after close scrutiny, recognized who the hirsute, ill-clad men who stood before him were." Once their identity became apparent, Alexander asked anxiously about the galleys. When Nearchus assured him that they were safely drawn up on the beach, where his sailors were making the necessary repairs and awaiting instructions, the King wept "tears of joy for the salvation of his fleet." He had given it up for lost.

Alexander himself had scarcely recovered from the rigors of leading 15,000 men on horses and 120,000 on foot across the desert wastes of Pakistan and Persia; nevertheless, he declared that he felt happier at receiving Nearchus' report "than in being the conqueror of all Asia." He now proposed that Nearchus continue with him to their headquarters at Babylon; another officer could be sent to command the fleet for the rest of the voyage to the planned rendezvous at Susa. But Nearchus insisted on returning to his sailors and his ships. "It is my duty, O King," he said simply, and went on his way.

Nearchus took nearly two months to reach Susa; he found Alexander there waiting for him. The exact date of their reunion is not known, but it was probably in February of 324 B.C. The expedition then headed overland to Babylon, where Alexander was struck down by a fever. The ancient world's most extraordinary conqueror died on June 13, 323 B.C., at the age of 32.

For centuries past, Indian, Persian and Arabian traders had been sailing between the Persian Gulf and India. But it was Nearchus' 1,000-mile, five-month passage that revealed for the Greeks this crucial sea link

On this Greek medallion, a fearless Alexander the Great charges elephant-borne warriors in the north of India in 326 B.C. At first, the lumbering beasts threatened to rout Alexander's cavalry, but the Greek infantry stampeded the elephants, and Alexander's forces then swept the Indians from the field.

between the Mediterranean world and eastern Asia. His journal of the voyage was so detailed that any ship captain could use it for navigating the route—and many later did.

For now, however, power struggles overshadowed commercial expansion. Alexander's leading generals split the newly won empire into three parts: Antigonus took over Macedonia and Greece, Ptolemy claimed Egypt, and Seleucus appropriated Syria and Asia Minor.

Ptolemy was able to seize most of Alexander's fleet, and with it he sought to make Egypt the leading sea power. But Antigonus was equally determined that Greece not be reduced to a second-class maritime state. So began one of history's first naval arms races. In the course of their wasteful competition, both sides built larger and larger ships: quadriremes, quinqueremes, sixers, seveners, and on up to a sixteener—a giant that had a grand total of 1,800 men at the oars.

For more than half a century these majestic warships fought a series of sea battles as Ptolemy, Antigonus and their heirs struggled for control of the eastern Mediterranean. Antigonus' son Demetrius was the most astute strategist, as he proved in 306 B.C. during a battle with an Egyptian fleet off another Salamis—this one a city on the south coast of Cyprus. In an engagement involving nearly 300 warships, Demetrius deliberately formed an unbalanced line, so that the battle gradually swung in a wide circle until he had maneuvered his ships between Ptolemy's fleet and the shore, thereby cutting it off from its onshore reserves. Ptolemy, realizing that his oarsmen were exhausted after hours of rowing, broke away; Demetrius then mopped up the scattered Egyptian vessels, capturing 120 of them.

Demetrius dominated the eastern half of the Mediterranean for the next two decades, until political turmoil in Greece brought him down. Thereafter, the balance of sea power in the area swung to the Egyptians, although Demetrius' son inflicted two defeats on them in the middle of the Third Century B.C. In truth, though, both navies had begun to lose their vigor by then. The dinosaurian galleys that each side relied on were simply too expensive to man and maintain, and before long they faded into extinction. In 168 B.C. one of Demetrius' cumbersome sixteeners was discovered rotting in its Macedonian dockyard; it had not been to sea for 70 years.

Even as warships clashed repeatedly and inconclusively in the eastern Mediterranean, the region's commerce grew richer and more diverse. To local products were now added those from the Asian lands that Alexander's conquests had opened up to Greek traders. Mediterranean ports expanded to become spectacular marinas protected from the surf by long man-made breakwaters; stone quays and impressive warehouses lined the inner harbors.

No port was more imposing than the one that Alexander had founded in Egypt and honored with his name—and in which he now lay entombed. Alexandria—Greek, or Hellenistic, in culture—beckoned to merchantmen with a 400-foot-tall lighthouse. Its wharves could accommodate 1,200 ships at a time *(pages 92-93)*. Other ships rode at anchor in the wide harbor, waiting to unload timber and metal, horses and marble, wool and wine, honey and dyes. The cargo list of two small vessels from

Syria has survived, preserved by Egypt's dry sand where it had been discarded in the Third Century B.C. Their freight included 450 gallons of table wine, 35 gallons of dessert wine, 10 amphorae of wild boar meat, along with two baskets of sponges and jars of figs, olive oil, honey, nuts, cheese, goat meat and venison.

Egypt by now had become the breadbasket of the Mediterranean world, and the Ptolemies could easily maintain a favorable balance of trade: Every captain was assured of a full hold of grain on his departure. Alexandria also became the key port for transshipment of all the products of Arabia and Somaliland. From these lands came frankincense, myrrh and ivory. From India flowed cosmetics, tortoise shell and such spices as cinnamon and pepper. One import was brought in solely for use by the Egyptian army: elephants, caught along the east coast of Africa. The exotic beasts received their training in warfare at a special camp near Alexandria.

For centuries, trade with the Orient had involved long caravan treks across Persia and Asia Minor. The Ptolemies now opened an all-sea route to India via the Red Sea, the Arabian Gulf and the Indian Ocean. And the Red Sea segment of the route was patrolled by the Egyptian navy to clear it of the pirates who had infested the area since the dawn of merchant seafaring.

As for the Mediterranean, its commerce was bolstered by the construction of larger vessels. The average merchant ship now carried 250 tons, the largest 1,000 or more. Rocking over the waves like massive sea cradles, some with figureheads on their rounded bows, these commercial vessels transported not only merchandise but passengers as well, the majority of them Mediterranean traders constantly on the move from market to market. To the single square sail of earlier vessels, the newer craft added a bowsprit square sail, which was raked forward and used primarily as an aid to steering. Many vessels also carried a triangular topsail, set above the main. And the largest freighters mounted an *epidromos*, a mizzen sail at the stern to catch more wind. Such trading vessels crowded not only Alexandria but also Tyre, Sidon, Ephesus, Gaza, Byblos, Rhodes and other port cities throughout the eastern reaches of the great sea.

And what of the West? There, during much of this period, a new state was flexing its maritime muscle. Around 200 B.C. its warships would enter the power struggles that were Alexander's legacy to the East. These upstarts, destined to dominate all of the Mediterranean for centuries to come, were the Romans.

The Colossus of Rhodes, a huge statue of the sun-god Helios that dominated the harbor entrance to the island port, is the centerpiece of a 17th Century French tapestry. During the Third and Second Centuries B.C., Rhodes traded with all the eastern Mediterranean ports. The Colossus was toppled by an earthquake in 226 B.C.

Alexandria: crossroads of the ancient world

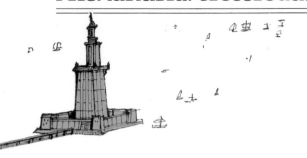

The grandest port in the world during the last three centuries before Christ was Alexandria. Strategically situated near the southeastern corner of the Mediterranean, the city became the natural transfer point for merchandise traveling to and from the East by way of the Nile and a short overland route to the Red Sea.

A merchantman bound for Alexandria was guided to the harbor by its great 400-foot Pharos lighthouse *(above)*, whose fire beacon could be seen 30 miles away. Passing through the opening in the breakwaters, the merchantman glided across the deep waters of the Great Harbor toward a sprawling metropolis. To the ship's left was the Palace Quarter of the ruling Ptolemies, with a Greek-style open theater *(top)*, zoological gardens and a library that, with more than half a million papyrus-roll books, had no equal.

Straight ahead were the colonnaded buildings of the Emporium, where most vessels disgorged and took on cargoes; these goods were shipped across the city to and from a lake that connected with the Nile *(pages 94-95)*. Traffic in the port was so heavy that, before tying up at the Emporium, a merchantman might spend days waiting in designated anchorages—suggested here by buoy-borne lines extending outward from the waterfront.

Grain was an especially high-priority cargo and followed a slightly different route. Empty grain ships continued through a dike opening to Alexandria's inner harbor *(bottom center)*, where they met barges that brought Egypt's harvest to Alexandria by way of a short canal from the lake.

This drawing, based on contemporary descriptions, is an artist's reconstruction of Alexandria as it might have looked at the height of its splendor. After Egypt's conquest by Rome and the subsequent breakup of the Roman Empire, Alexandria went into a long decline. During the Middle Ages its buildings were cannibalized for their marble, and earthquakes toppled what was left. The once-proud city's remains now lie buried beneath the modern metropolis.

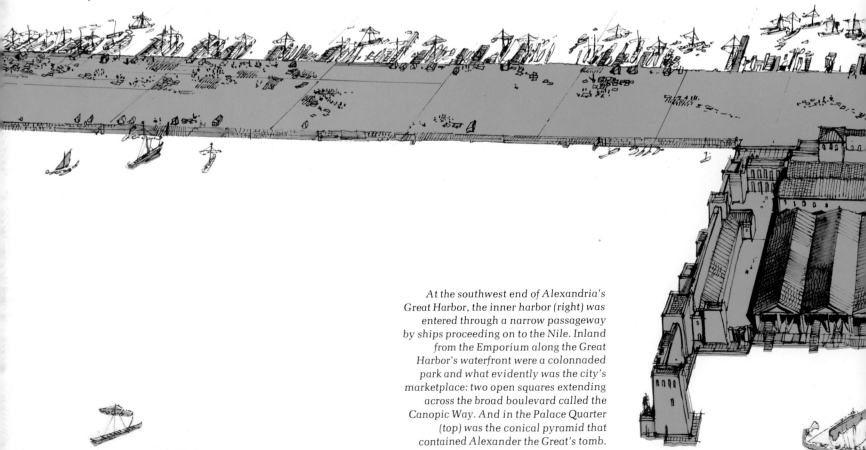

At the southwest end of Alexandria's Great Harbor, the inner harbor (right) was entered through a narrow passageway by ships proceeding on to the Nile. Inland from the Emporium along the Great Harbor's waterfront were a colonnaded park and what evidently was the city's marketplace: two open squares extending across the broad boulevard called the Canopic Way. And in the Palace Quarter (top) was the conical pyramid that contained Alexander the Great's tomb.

Just as Alexandria's Great Harbor gave the city access to the Mediterranean, the eastern trade routes were made accessible by Lake Mareotis, which bounded the city on its inland side and was connected by canal to the Nile *(map, bottom right).*

This drawing shows the northeastern reaches of the lake, with an imagined example of one of the Ptolemies' many toll stations. At top, cargo vessels are seen approaching and leaving the wharves of the city. In the foreground, other ships lie at anchor, awaiting clearance at the toll station. The typical station complex would have included a collector's office *(far end of the wharf),* barracks for troops, and a colonnaded warehouse for goods on which payments were due. On the waterfront and on the canal shore at left are houses for toll-station workers and other villagers.

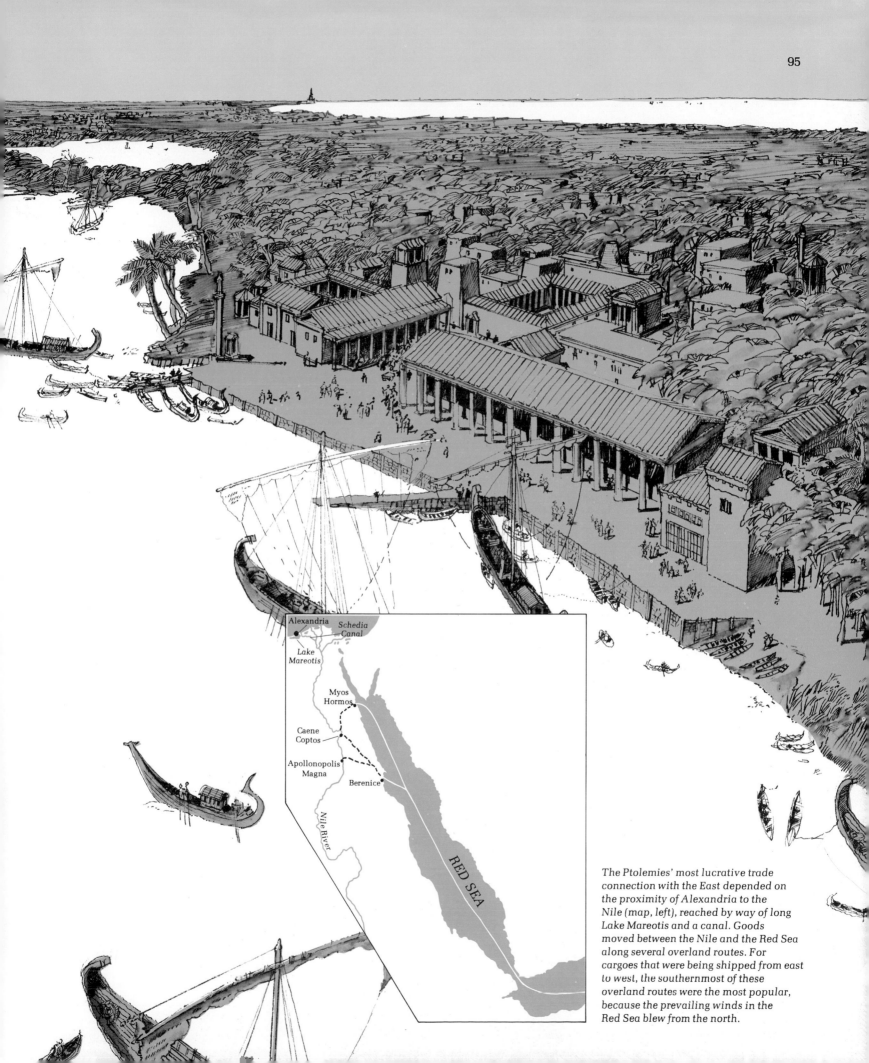

Alexandria
Schedia Canal

Lake Mareotis

Myos Hormos

Caene Coptos

Apollonopolis Magna

Berenice

Nile River

RED SEA

The Ptolemies' most lucrative trade connection with the East depended on the proximity of Alexandria to the Nile (map, left), reached by way of long Lake Mareotis and a canal. Goods moved between the Nile and the Red Sea along several overland routes. For cargoes that were being shipped from east to west, the southernmost of these overland routes were the most popular, because the prevailing winds in the Red Sea blew from the north.

With the income from Egypt's sales of grain and other commodities, plus the ceaseless flow of revenues from toll collections, the Ptolemies could indulge almost any whim. None spent more freely than Ptolemy IV, who ruled in the Third Century B.C. Among his fancies were vessels of a size never dreamed of before, including an elephantine war galley called a "forty" (pages 72-73) and a magnificent royal barge, here recreated from ancient descriptions. The floating palace was used for entertaining as well as for business of state, and it put in at ports on the Nile so that Ptolemy could overawe subjects throughout his rich kingdom.

Ptolemy IV's royal barge, fitted with a pair of shrines at her double prow, was 300 feet long, 45 feet wide and towered more than 60 feet above the water. Soaring columns surrounded an entranceway leading to a huge banquet hall. This majestic reception room was paneled with split cedar and Milesian cypress, ringed by a frieze of gold and ivory, and furnished with 20 couches for reclining guests. Doors adorned with gold and ivory led to a transverse passageway separating the men's from the women's quarters. The royal barge floated on the Nile's current or was towed against it by dozens of oared galleys.

Chapter 4

Soldiers of the sea

he Roman navy that entered the eastern Mediterranean in 201 B.C. was a formidable force, yet it was also a new one. For much of their history, the Romans were farmers, cattle ranchers, foot soldiers—and landlubbers. Beginning about 500 B.C., they had marched forth from their original settlement on the banks of the Tiber River, subduing the mountaineers of the Apennines and the peoples of the plains, including Greeks who had colonized southern Italy. Over the next two centuries, Rome knit together these confused areas under a system of government—an oligarchical senate, popular assemblies, and a hierarchy of magistrates—that was dynamic, conscientious and (for its day) democratic.

Throughout this period, the strength of Rome lay in its army. The sea belonged to the heirs of Alexander, and—especially in the west—to the Carthaginians, descendants of the Phoenicians. Even as the Romans had expanded and consolidated their power on land, the onetime Phoenician colony on the North African coast had built a great maritime empire, acquiring ports that stretched from Tangier to Tripoli on the shore of present-day Libya, and establishing garrison outposts in Spain (controlling the silver mines of the hinterland) as well as in Sardinia and western Sicily.

For all their aggressive inclinations, the Romans seemed hopelessly ill-equipped to match the maritime might of Carthage. Rome had possessed no navy at all until 311 B.C., when two 10-galley fleets were organized—mainly for the protection of coastal towns from pirates. Such naval operations as the Republic first mounted were inglorious. In 310 one of the little fleets made an amphibious raid to put down a rebellion near Pompeii; the marines were ignominiously routed and fled back to their ships, and the veteran Roman army had to be called in to subdue the rebels two years later. In 282 the galleys sailed down the coast to attack the Greek town of Tarentum, inside the heel of the Italian boot; the fleet was crushed, and again the army had to complete the conquest. For nearly 20 years after this debacle, the little Roman navy rotted away in its sheds; and by 264 B.C. the Romans did not have a single serviceable galley.

In that year, the conflicting interests of Carthage and Rome reached a flash point when the Roman army crossed the Strait of Messina in troop transports and landed on Sicily. For the next 23 years the two powers would struggle for mastery of the island. Improbably, that conflict, known as the First Punic War (*Punicas* was the Latin word for Phoenicians), was to be fought mostly on the sea.

By 260 B.C. the Roman armies had swept across Sicily's mountainous terrain, meeting no serious obstacle until they approached the southern shores of the island. Polybius, a Greek historian transplanted to Rome, recorded that while many of the inland towns "joined the Romans from dread of their land forces, yet a still larger number of seaboard towns held aloof from them in terror of the Carthaginian fleet."

So in the spring of 260 the Roman Senate issued an astonishing decree. A nation that possessed not a single warship—"without any resources for it at all," wrote Polybius, "and without having ever entertained an idea of naval war"—was called upon to build 100 quinque-

This bronze image of Minerva, goddess of war, adorned the prow of a Roman war galley. The head, dating from the First Century B.C., was found in the waters off Actium in Greece, and could be a relic of the epic battle between the rival Roman navies of Mark Antony and Octavian.

remes and 20 triremes within 60 days. Quinqueremes were the backbone of the Carthaginian fleet; and with nothing to match them, the Senators realized, the Romans would be defeated before they began.

Rome had no shipwrights capable of carrying out the Senators' orders—the Republic had never owned a quinquereme—and scarcely a trained oarsman or sailor. However, the Greek cities of southern Italy that had fallen under Roman control were old in the ways of the sea, and it was to them that Rome must now have turned. Even these cities had never built a quinquereme, but happenstance provided a prototype. The Carthaginians had recently attacked some Roman troop transports in the Strait of Messina. One of their quinqueremes, wrote Polybius, "charged so furiously that it ran aground, and falling into the hands of the Romans served them as a model on which they constructed their whole fleet." These swift, maneuverable ships required expert crews, so Rome did not attempt to duplicate them exactly. By a mixture of design and clumsiness, the shipwrights produced quinqueremes that were slower yet more robust than those of Carthage—a landlubberly fleet of floating infantry carriers, built of unseasoned wood.

An intensive search for oarsmen now began; the fleet required more than 30,000. The citizens of Rome itself were considered to be above such servitude, but the tough farmers and herdsmen of the Italian interior were not. The legend of Roman "galley slaves" is merely a legend; the Roman galleys' oars were always pulled by freemen. In bewildered droves, farm boys were crowded onto makeshift rowing benches set up on land, and trained to pull to the chant of the time beater. While they sweated in unison, the shipbuilders hammered and jointed and calked the fleet together at such a prodigious rate that in only two months' time the huge, gauche armada of 120 ships was complete, and its raw crews were tumbled onto the rowing benches. Cursing, retching, stammering fearful pleas to their country gods, they rowed out for a brief practice on the real sea. The whole miracle was accomplished almost before the Carthaginians realized it.

In June of 260 this fleet left the Tiber and lumbered down the southwest coast to reassemble at Syracuse in Sicily. And here, as the fleet lay at anchor, some brilliant innovator—no one knows who—produced a revolutionary device for warfare at sea. Pondering the problem of the Carthaginians' superior speed and maneuverability, this anonymous inventor designed what came to be known as a *corvus*, or raven—a 36-foot-long boarding bridge that dangled threateningly from a tall pole at the prow of each ship. Each of these ravens was suspended by a block and tackle, and could be swiveled sideways from its pole head. At the end of each gangway projected an iron spike. When the tackle was released, the bridge would come crashing down on the enemy from a height of some 20 feet; the raven's iron bill would embed itself in the enemy's deck, holding the galley fast while the Romans stormed over the causeway two abreast. In an attack conducted in this way rather than by ramming or with missiles, manpower would be all important; each Roman galley therefore added 80 crack legionnaires to its normal complement of 40 armed marines.

Meanwhile, the Carthaginians, not content simply to protect their

*An imaginative French engraving from the
18th Century pictures the Roman raven
as a gangway suspended over the bow of
a warship and tipped by an elaborate,
weighted grapnel. No contemporary
Roman illustration of the revolutionary
boarding device is known to survive.*

towns along Sicily's southern and western shores, were ravaging the island's northern coast with a fleet of 130 war galleys. When their captains sighted the new Roman navy plodding through the Strait of Messina to put a stop to their depredations, they regarded it with amused disdain. Their own fleet was slightly outnumbered; the 120 galleys commissioned by the Roman Senate had been bolstered by 25 more, hastily constructed by some of the other Italian towns. But the Carthaginian fleet included more quinqueremes; and they were the finest of their day, superbly rowed by veteran oarsmen.

The commander of the Carthaginian fleet was a mediocre admiral named Hannibal—not the later, more famous bearer of this popular Carthaginian name. As he watched the enemy come wallowing out to battle off the Sicilian coast near Mylae, Hannibal was overjoyed. The Romans appeared to be offering themselves up for sacrifice. The ponderous galleys—their blades flailing the water as the green oarsmen tried to keep their unison, their decks jammed with armor-clad infantry, their bows dangling the gawky ravens—presented an outlandish sight. Hannibal was so confident of victory that he did not even bother to form battle order. Like descending pirates, the Carthaginians swept into the Roman fleet, ready to ram and veer away in the time-tested tactics of battle at sea.

Commanding the Roman fleet was Consul Caius Duilius, a fighter more accustomed to infantry combat. Determined to turn the contest into man-to-man battle as soon as possible, Duilius led his galleys head on into the advancing enemy. And as the Carthaginian ships struck, the ravens descended.

They thundered onto the enemy decks like giant hands, and their grip held sure. The Roman oarsmen quickly backed water to prevent the ravens' iron beaks from being wrenched away. The fleets became a congested mass, ship bound to ship by the ponderous gangways. Showers of javelins and arrows rattled over the decks. And with their four-foot-long shields held before them like a wall, the Roman marines and legionnaires charged across the wooden bridges.

The Carthaginian forces, composed of mercenaries—Libyans, Gauls and Spaniards under Carthaginian commanders, as was the Carthaginian custom—were trained in ship-killing tactics, not to fight man-to-man on deck. They gave way in shock and amazement. The Romans, sheathed in bronze greaves, breastpieces and helmets, swept onto the Carthaginian decks, their short swords stabbing through the enemy's light armor. Wrote Polybius: "Some of the Carthaginians were cut down, while others surrendered in bewildered terror at the battle in which they found themselves engaged"; it was, he said, "exactly like a land fight."

Those who tried to fight back were met by an invincible rampart of Roman shields, bossed and bound in iron, behind which the legionary helmets, topped by plumes of feathers, appeared to double the size of the men. When the first wave of the Carthaginian ships withdrew, they found that they had lost 30 galleys. Even Hannibal's flagship had been boarded and taken. However, the admiral himself had made a daring but ignominious escape in a skiff.

More circumspectly now, the Carthaginian quinqueremes reassem-

Rome erected this triumphal column to honor Caius Duilius, who commanded the Republic's navy in its first victory in 260 B.C. The column is decorated with carved anchors and displays the prows of six Carthaginian galleys that were captured in the battle off Sicily.

bled and advanced again. This time, wary of the ravens, they tried to run around the Roman flanks and attack the cumbersome galleys broadside or astern. But Duilius, whose ships now outnumbered the Carthaginians by almost three to two, had backed up his front with a second line. As the Carthaginians darted in on the first rank, the second row of ships pushed forward with the fearsome ravens hovering on their prows. Again the bridges came crashing down on the Carthaginian decks, and again the Roman soldiers swept across their causeways, hacking down everyone in their path. This time the Carthaginians fled. They left behind 44 ships sunk and captured, with a loss of 10,000 men; the Romans' loss is unrecorded, but was certainly far less.

Duilius had won his country's first naval victory. He was granted a triumphal procession and a lavish memorial in Rome. "He was the first to fit out and train ships and crews," declared the monument, "and, with these, he defeated in battle on the high seas all the Carthaginian ships and their mighty naval personnel"—certainly a novel testimonial for a Roman soldier.

The Romans could not follow up their first naval victory by conquering the enemy towns in Sicily, which were heavily fortified and supplied by a reinforced Carthaginian fleet. But shortly afterward, Hannibal, attempting to provision Carthage's outposts on the island of Sardinia, was surprised in harbor by a Roman fleet that destroyed many of his vessels. His sailors, exasperated by their admiral's bumbling leadership, mutinied and killed him in the customary Carthaginian manner, nailing him to a cross.

Four years later the Romans decided they were strong enough to strike at the very heart of the Carthaginians' empire, their capital on the coast of North Africa. Rome by then had a fleet of 330 quinqueremes; Carthage had rebuilt its navy to 350. The risks for Rome were huge. Success depended on the Roman navy. Isolated from their homeland by the breadth of the Mediterranean, and invading a populous land where no friendly harbor awaited them, the Romans would first have to cripple the Carthaginian fleet.

Early that summer the carefully prepared Roman armada, together with some 80 triremes converted into horse transports, left its home port of Ostia and sailed south to cast anchor near the town of Ecnomus on the southern coast of Sicily. Here the marines on board were buttressed by soldiers who had been occupying the island, raising the fleet's total fighting force to 39,600 men.

One morning that summer, probably at sunrise, the Romans embarked and set sail along the coast, heading for the western end of the island before turning south toward Carthage. The Carthaginians were positioned squarely across their path at Heraclea, about 35 miles west of Ecnomus. The Carthaginian commanders, probably warned of the Roman advance by fire signals from observers along the shore, assembled their men and addressed them ardently on the importance of the battle ahead. If they won, their leaders pointed out, the war would be confined to Sicily. But if they lost, they would be thrown back to the North African coast. So "they put to sea," wrote Polybius, "in the full fervor of excited gallantry."

The two fleets met on calm waters in the clear light of morning. The Romans, under Consuls Marcus Atilius Regulus and Lucius Manlius Vulso, moved forward in an enormous wedge formation. At the wedge's point the consuls sailed side by side in their sixer flagships, while behind them the spearhead of the fleet fanned back in two long battle lines. The rear of the wedge was closed by a line of some 70 quinqueremes; in front of that line, protected on all sides, another line of 80 quinqueremes towed the clumsy and precarious horse transports.

The luckless Hannibal had been succeeded by a capable and experienced Carthaginian admiral named Hamilcar. Studying the Roman fleet, he deployed his 350 quinqueremes with rapid expertise. He had immediately realized that the Romans' horse transports lent their fleet a glaring vulnerability, hindering the galleys towing them and—if they were to be protected—slowing the fleet as a whole. Hamilcar plotted his strategy accordingly. He sent a quarter of his fleet to form a left wing along the Sicilian shore. To the right he dispatched a force of fast quinqueremes, under the command of his experienced captain Hanno. These movements left his center weak—as he planned.

The Roman fleet, massed in a powerful but inflexible battle order under swaying ravens, forged on toward the waiting Carthaginians. Seeing the thin, extended center of the Carthaginian line, the Roman commanders ordered a head-on attack. The Roman galleys at the apex of the wedge, followed by two lines of ships on either side, charged forward. At once the Carthaginian center retreated, backing water or turning in feigned flight, while the Carthaginian flanks spread out on either side of the Roman wedge.

Now was Hamilcar's moment. His plan was to close his flanks in a giant pincer action, crushing the Romans in a deadly embrace. He signaled his captains to move to the attack. Instantly the Carthaginian center turned to confront its pursuers, and the two wings swept down to encircle the foe.

But the aspect of the battle had undergone a critical change in the minutes since Regulus and Vulso had ordered their attack on the Carthaginian center. Whether by blunder or design—scholars have debated the question ever since—the Roman galleys towing the transports, together with the protective squadron of quinqueremes at the rear of the wedge, did not follow the leading edge of the Roman fleet in its attack. They lagged behind. So instead of holding to the formation of a solid triangle, the Roman fleet had separated into two elements, with a wide gap between them. Hamilcar's enveloping strategy was thus thrown into disarray.

The protective squadron of the Roman rear turned seaward to meet Hanno and his Carthaginian right wing. At the same time, the captains towing the Roman transports dropped their hawsers and moved to challenge the attackers coming from the other side. The single battle that had started with one fleet encircling the other became, instead, three separate battles. Meanwhile, the Roman transports drifted out to sea before a northeasterly wind, their terrified horses stamping and whinnying in the holds.

In the separate encounters, the Romans' headlong courage became more important than clever seamanship. The galleys that had cast off their transports rushed toward the shore, where they turned their sterns to the beach and formed a crescent, prows outward like a herd of beasts under attack. Dangling their predatory ravens, they dared the enemy to come on. The Carthaginian center, overpowered by the spearhead of what had been the Roman wedge, was first to give way. Latched to their heavy attackers by the ravens, they were unable to maneuver. Their sailors, too lightly armed to fend off the Roman legionnaires swarming across the footbridges, were forced back against the bulwarks, then driven over the side or cut down.

Leaving Vulso to mop up the last vessels of the Carthaginian center, Regulus turned his flotilla about and went to the aid of the Roman rear, which was engaging Hanno's quinqueremes. Regulus came upon Hanno from behind, and the Carthaginian right wing was caught in a vise. Before he was completely surrounded, Hanno, who had the fastest quinqueremes in the Carthaginian fleet, skillfully withdrew the remains of his squadron to the open sea.

Once more the robustness of Rome had been too great for the nimbleness of Carthage on the sea. In contrast to Roman casualties of 24 ships sunk in the battle off Ecnomus, more than one quarter of the Carthaginian fleet of 350 was lost: 64 were captured by their foe and more than 30 sent to the bottom.

Yet a stunning setback lay in store for the Romans. They wanted to follow up the victory at Ecnomus with a swift pursuit of the enemy fleet as it withdrew toward Africa, but the exhaustion of their rowers and the necessity of refitting for a completely new enterprise—nothing less than the invasion of Africa—required a period of rest. By the time the Roman force arrived in Carthaginian waters, the winter was almost upon them; it was decided to send all but 40 ships of the fleet home and leave the army to prepare the ground for an all-out attack on the city of Carthage in the early summer of 255. Under Regulus, 25,500 men, including about 500 cavalry, took over the Punic coastal town of Aspis, scoured the countryside for winter provisions and flexed their muscles with raids and patrols.

For reasons not explained by ancient chroniclers, Regulus engaged the Carthaginians in early spring, before the Roman fleet had returned to Africa for the climactic combined assault. On the plains before Carthage, the Roman soldiery was shattered by Carthaginian war elephants and cavalry—which outnumbered Regulus' horsemen 8 to 1. Regulus and about 500 legionnaires were captured; about 2,000 retreated to Aspis; the rest of the 25,500 were slaughtered.

In the Roman Senate, the question of rescuing the survivors in Aspis became the subject of a bitter debate. News of Regulus' disaster had so shocked some Romans that they wanted nothing more to do with an African adventure, and even favored leaving the remnants of the expeditionary force to die in Africa. Other voices urged a rescue by the navy, and one Senator warned that if Rome "left those brave men to their fate, the Roman people would utterly disgrace themselves in the eyes of the whole world."

Those who favored a relief expedition won out. The fleet returned and,

Tactical triumph off Ecnomus

When the fledgling Roman navy met its veteran Carthaginian counterpart off Ecnomus on the coast of Sicily in 256 B.C., the result was the first major Roman victory won chiefly by tactics. As shown in the sequence of diagrams below, the key to the battle was the Romans' instantaneous reaction—perhaps by accident, perhaps by design—to the Carthaginians' own tactics. The latter, confronting a temptingly solid formation of Roman ships, attempted to encircle the enemy. But the Roman fleet immediately separated into three units and pulled apart the Carthaginian fleet in the process. Having destroyed the momentum and unity of the Carthaginians, the Romans then proceeded to attack their

Foiling an encirclement

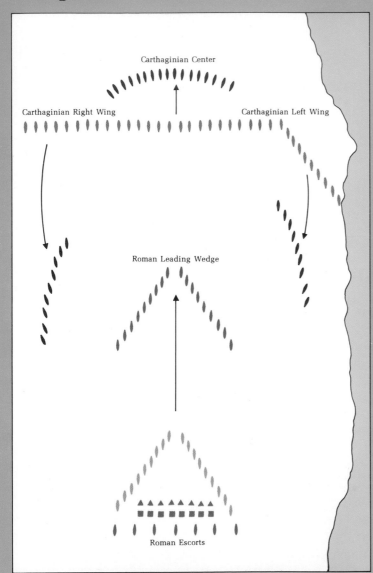

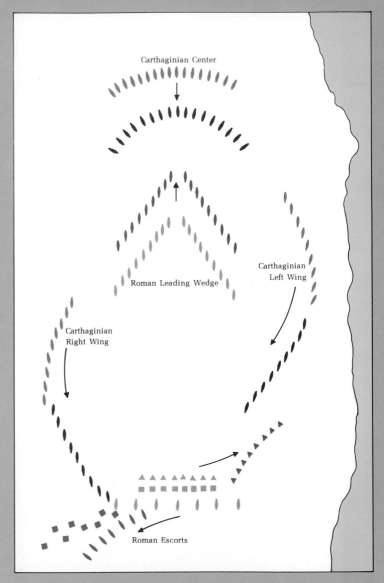

As the Roman fleet off Ecnomus advances in a triangular formation (bottom), the Carthaginian ships range themselves in line-abreast formation. They then send their wings outside the Roman flanks to encircle them. The Carthaginian center meanwhile feigns retreat (top). The Roman wedge obligingly speeds after the retreating foe, leaving the fleet's slow-moving transports, with their escorts and tow ships, astern.

While the Carthaginian wings continue their encircling movement, the center of the fleet turns forward to engage the oncoming Roman wedge. Meanwhile, to the surprise of the Carthaginians, the Roman formation disperses even further: The transports' escorts wheel to face the Carthaginian right wing, and the tow ships cut the transports adrift and run toward shore in order to hold off the other Carthaginian wing.

107

enemy piecemeal and overwhelm them by sheer strength.

In the diagrams, the Roman vessels are shown in blue, the Carthaginian galleys in red. The symbols represent contingents of ships rather than individual vessels (in reality, 330 Roman ships encountered 350 Carthaginian vessels). Oblongs stand for fighting galleys; squares indicate towed Ro-

man transport vessels, laden with horses; triangles are their tow ships. Most of the Roman and Carthaginian units are shown twice in each diagram—lighter-colored symbols show their earlier positions in each illustrated battle sequence, darker-colored symbols mark their later positions. The arrows show the direction of the vessels' movements.

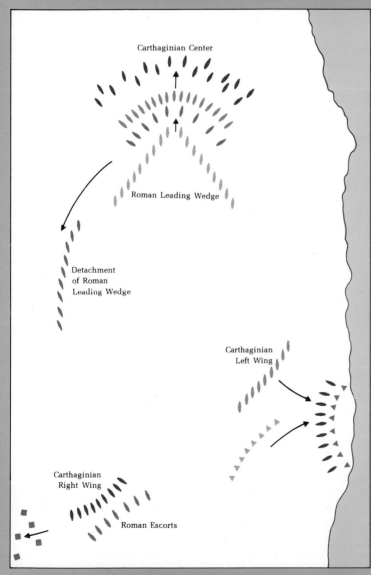

The battle has now broken up into three detached encounters, disrupting the Carthaginian strategy of encirclement. In the engagement of the two center contingents (top), the Romans overwhelm the weaker Carthaginian line and are able to detach a unit to aid the transport escorts in their struggle against the Carthaginian right wing. Near the shore, the Roman tow ships are backed against the beach by Carthaginian forces.

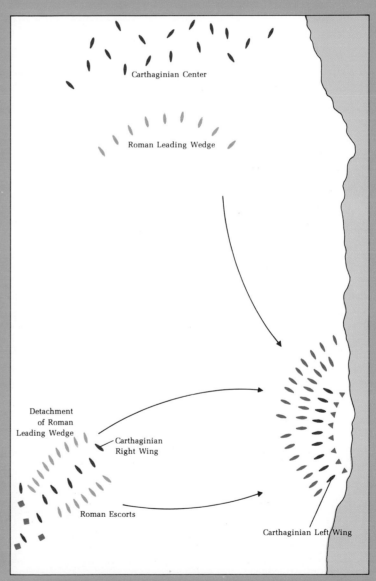

The battle is decided as the defeated Carthaginian center scatters (top) and the Carthaginian right wing flees out to sea. Roman forces thus released now move against the rear of the Carthaginians, pinning the tow ships against the beach. They are joined by parts of the Roman leading wedge. Crushed in a nutcracker, the Carthaginians are sunk or captured, freeing the Romans to rescue their drifting transports.

reinforced by the 40 vessels that had been left behind in Africa in the preceding autumn, engaged the enfeebled Punic navy. Few details of the battle have emerged from ancient accounts; but by its conclusion the Romans had managed to capture 114 Carthaginian ships virtually undamaged, crews and all. Only about 16 Carthaginian vessels were destroyed during the encounter; the Carthaginians apparently allowed themselves to be trapped close to shore, and many of their vessels were simply driven onto the beach.

Filled out by its Carthaginian prizes, a prodigious Roman fleet of 464 war galleys and numerous horse transports soon afterward reached the waters off the southern coast of Sicily in July. Then came disaster—a disaster too total for men to have inflicted on one another. Yet men played their part: "Fortune was not so much to blame as the commanders themselves," wrote the historian Polybius. The consuls who led the fleet were constantly warned by their pilots not to push along the exposed southern Sicilian coast. Not only were the shores harborless, but, as the pilots pointed out, the area was notoriously susceptible to sudden storms "between the rising of Orion and that of the Dog Star"—that is, from June 28 to July 26.

The consuls ignored the warnings: They had no appreciation of the power of a storm at sea, and in any case, they were intent on overawing Carthaginian coastal cities along their way. As Polybius explained, "It is a peculiarity of the Roman people as a whole to treat everything as a question of main strength; to consider that they must of course accomplish whatever they have proposed to themselves; and that nothing is impossible that they have once determined upon." That was all very well on land, he said, where their only adversaries were men. "But to contend with the sea and sky is to fight against a force immeasurably superior to their own."

The storm hit the Romans off the craggy coast of Camarina. The enormous fleet, shambling eastward with its transport ships and unwieldy galleys, was driven onto the rocks. The tempest may have been no more than one of the hard westerly winds that often strike the Sicilian coast in midsummer. But for the low-built warships, it was catastrophic. First they stowed their wind-ripped sails; then, as the waves mounted, they blocked their oar ports to keep from being flooded. With neither sails nor oars, the galleys were at the mercy of the storm. The seas came over the bulwarks, sweeping marines and soldiers overboard and pouring below decks to drown the oarsmen on their benches. The unwieldy ravens were a lethal handicap now; the top-heavy galleys lurched wildly, many of them foundering. And in the transports, thousands of Carthaginian prisoners, captured at sea, waited in helpless terror until their vessels sank under the waves.

Other ships were dashed against the rocks, "where they went to pieces," wrote Polybius, "and filled all the seaboard with corpses and wreckage." So numerous were the Carthaginian prizes that the whole fleet was probably fatally undermanned. The losses were the greatest yet suffered by a fleet on the sea. Of the 464 war galleys and scores of transport ships, only 80 survived. No ancient historian ventured to count the dead, who must have numbered some 100,000 men.

Fighting men line the deck of a two-banked war galley carved on a Roman tomb. Besides the shields and spears carried by these men, Roman marines were equipped with swords and grapnels.

Yet such was the resilience of the Romans that they immediately proceeded to build a new fleet, and with astonishing speed. During the winter of 255-254, they constructed 140 galleys. Later in the year, these ships joined the remnant of 80 that had ridden out the previous summer's storm, and attacked and subdued Carthaginian towns in Sicily. But fate seemed to have turned against Rome. In 253, as the fleet was returning from Sicily under the consul Caius Sempronius Blaesus, it was struck by storm again. Of its 200 ships, more than 150 went to the bottom with tens of thousands of trained rowers and soldiers, or were dashed to bits against the southern shore of Italy.

From this blow even the Romans took time to recover. They did not resume naval warfare against Carthage until the summer of 250 B.C., when some 120 war galleys blockaded Lilybaeum, Carthage's chief stronghold in Sicily, while a Roman army pressed in by land. But the tide seemed still to be running in favor of the Carthaginians. Their agile ships continually outmaneuvered the clumsy Roman galleys, running the blockade to supply their besieged city. And one day a Carthaginian fleet of 50 galleys swept down on the Romans before a powerful following wind and temporarily lifted the blockade entirely. "Partly from astonishment at this sudden appearance," wrote Polybius, "partly from dread of being carried along with the enemy by the violence of the gale into the harbor of their opponents, the Romans did not venture to ob-struct the entrance of the reinforcement, but stood out at sea overpow-ered with amazement at the audacity of the enemy."

Worse was to come. The Romans had scarcely succeeded in reestab-lishing their blockade when a single galley captained by another Hanni-bal, called "the Rhodian" from his place of origin, ran right through their line of ships and into the harbor in broad daylight. The insulted Romans reacted by positioning their 10 fastest vessels near the harbor mouth to catch Hannibal if he tried to come out in the same audacious fashion. Yet he did so with aplomb and—wrote Polybius—"not only sailed out without receiving any damage to ship or crew, scudding along the bows of the enemy as though they were fixed in their places, but even brought his ship to, after running a short way ahead, and, with his oars out and ready, seemed to challenge the foe to a contest. When none of them ventured to put out to attack him, because of the speed of his rowing, he sailed away: having thus with his one ship successfully defied the entire fleet of the enemy."

The humiliated Romans finally got their revenge when a swift Cartha-ginian quadrireme ran aground on the harbor mole and the blockaders captured it. In this vessel the Romans placed a picked crew of oarsmen and soldiers and lay in wait for Hannibal. The Rhodian sailed out from harbor in his usual insolent manner the very next day, and was startled to see the quadrireme bearing down on him. The Roman rowers over-hauled his galley, and he was taken prisoner.

The lesson was not lost on Hannibal's colleagues; efforts to run the Roman blockade came to a virtual halt. The Romans also learned a lesson from this experience, gradually changing their galley design from pon-derous troop carriers to faster, more maneuverable quinqueremes pat-terned on the Carthaginian craft. In the process, they abandoned their clumsy but effective raven. Evidently they considered that a boarding bridge would not be necessary in their new warship. And certainly the storm off Sicily had demonstrated the vulnerability of the raven-equipped galley. But to give it up so precipitately was a blunder, as the Romans now learned to their cost.

Their problem was compounded by a bullheaded leader in command of inexperienced oarsmen. In the summer of 249, a fleet of 120 Roman galleys formed up to attack a Carthaginian force of 100 vessels that lay at anchor in the Sicilian port of Drepanum. In Lilybaeum's harbor 12 miles away, the Roman Consul Publius Claudius Pulcher chafed to set sail against the enemy fleet before it escaped. But he reckoned without the fleet's augurs, priestly attendants without whose blessings no major Roman military decision was made. Augurs in turn received their guid-ance from birds—in this case, a flock of sacred chickens aboard the flagship. And now the augurs pointed to a bad omen for the expedition: The sacred chickens were not feeding.

"If they won't eat, they can drink," retorted Pulcher in a fury, and had them thrown overboard.

The Roman fleet set out near midnight, seeking the advantage of sur-prise. When the Roman galleys appeared over the horizon at dawn, the talented Carthaginian admiral Adherbal hastily assembled his forces

and outlined a plan for defense. Its key was the layout of the harbor of Drepanum, which had two entrances. Adherbal's men boarded their galleys and waited until Pulcher's fleet arrived. As Adherbal had hoped, the slow-witted Pulcher sent all his galleys through one entrance. The Carthaginian fleet promptly raced out through the other.

The Romans fell into confusion. By the time they realized what had happened, some of their ships were inside the harbor, others were pouring through the entrance and others, including Pulcher's flagship, were still outside. Pulcher at least had the sense to realize that he was being lured into the same trap the Carthaginians had been in. He ordered his galleys in the harbor to come out. They became entangled with other Roman vessels in the entrance, hulls bumping and oars snapping. At last they formed a ragged line outside the harbor, their sterns to the shore and their prows to the enemy. But now they lay so close to the shore that they had no room to maneuver.

The Carthaginians, swarming out of the harbor's other passage, swooped down on the huddled Roman front. But instead of charging in force, as the Romans would have preferred, Adherbal sent his galleys darting at the line, ramming and quickly retreating. Now the lack of ravens spelled the Romans' doom. Unable to grapple with the attackers, they could not send their marines onto the enemy's decks. Instead of the Romans' favorite form of combat—an infantry battle at sea—it was a classic ship-against-ship contest, at which the Carthaginians excelled. When one of the unwieldy Roman ships charged out of the line, it was immediately surrounded by quick Carthaginian galleys and cut off.

In a Pompeiian wall painting, Roman marines crowd the decks of four galleys. While the Romans adopted the ram-prowed warship design favored by navies in the Mediterranean since the First Millennium B.C., they always preferred to grapple and board rather than ram.

When a Roman vessel tried to slip around behind the line, it ran aground on the shoals along Sicily's shore.

Slowly the whole Roman line began to disintegrate. Many galleys were sunk; others became stranded on the shore, and their crews escaped into the interior. Pulcher fled with a mere 27 ships of his left wing, leaving 93 sunk or captured behind him, with 20,000 men lost.

The gods of weather delivered the death blow. Soon after the debacle off Drepanum, the Romans scraped together the last of their navy—120 galleys and 800 transports—and sent it to reinforce the blockade at Lilybaeum. En route, near the same Sicilian shore where a storm had wrecked a Roman fleet in 255, another tempest struck. The Carthaginians wisely anchored in the shelter of a tall headland; but the Romans were scattered to the winds and lost all but two of their ships. By the end of the year 249, the naval might of the Roman Republic had been reduced to a pitiful 20 galleys, and Carthage was once again mistress of the seas.

But only for a time. For five years the Romans "abandoned the sea," wrote Polybius. Meanwhile, the heavily fortified Carthaginian port cities of Sicily, supplied by sea, successfully held out against Rome's most determined attacks overland.

Because the Roman treasury was now impoverished, the Senate made an appeal to the country's leading citizens to fit out yet another fleet. So wealthy were these pillars of the Republic that a new 200-quinquereme Roman navy rose swiftly from the wreckage of the old, and by the year 242 B.C., Consul Gaius Lutatius Catulus was prepared to sail against the Carthaginians.

Catulus intercepted some 170 Carthaginian ships off Sicily's Aegates Islands and proceeded to engage in a classic ramming action. The enemy admiral, unprepared for a Roman fleet employing the Carthaginian method of sea warfare, was soundly beaten, and most of his armada was destroyed. He escaped to Carthage, where he met the customary fate of a defeated Carthaginian—on the cross. In the momentum of victory, Rome negotiated a treaty with Carthage. Thus, in 241 B.C., the First Punic War ended, with all of Sicily at last ceded to the republic on the banks of the Tiber.

During the succeeding century, Rome and Carthage fought two more Punic Wars. It was in the next one that the famous Hannibal, unable to attack the Italian coast because of Rome's superior fleet, was forced to land in Spain and lead his army, elephants and all, over the Alps; the expedition bogged down in the mountainous Italian terrain, and Hannibal eventually returned to Carthage in defeat. The last Punic war ended in disaster for the Carthaginians when the Roman navy blockaded their home city in North Africa and Roman soldiers then razed it. By 146 B.C., what had been the maritime capital of the Mediterranean world was a plowed field, its furrows sown with salt so that nothing would grow. Carthage would never endanger the Republic again.

Half a century earlier, a Rhodian galley had rowed up the Tiber to invite the Roman navy into the eastern Mediterranean. Ever since Alexander the Great's empire had been divided up, the island nation of Rhodes had been playing a delicate game, providing the balance of power between the larger warring factions of Macedonia and Egypt. But by the end of the Third Century B.C., the Egyptian navy had been neglected, and Macedonia's mighty fleet threatened to dominate the eastern reaches of the great sea—hence the Rhodian request for aid.

Rome responded with 50 of its swift new quinqueremes. Together with the Rhodian navy, they overwhelmed the Macedonians and compelled them to sue for peace. The Roman galleys then returned home; but the Romans had caught the Eastern virus. Here was rich new ground for their expanding empire, and they moved to exploit it—at the expense of their Rhodian ally.

Rome proceeded not by warfare but by astute commercial politics. In 167 B.C. the Romans acquired the island of Delos, which was strategically located in the midst of the eastern Mediterranean's trading nations. Then they ceded it to Athens, on condition that the island would be maintained as a free port, levying no customs duties. Within one year this free port had reduced the trade of Rhodes to a fraction of its previous level. The entire luxury traffic of the Mediterranean world—spices, incense, slaves—flooded into Delos, and Rhodes was limited to receiving grain and wine (largely because the heavy vessels carrying these commodities required Rhodes' deep harbor).

Delos became an entrepôt of Levantine dynamism and acumen. Greeks, Phoenicians, Syrians, Jews, Arabs—even merchants from the Red Sea and beyond—set up their offices there, and turned Delos into a port of Babel. ("Merchant, sail in and unload! Everything's as good as sold," ran a local saying.) And there Middle Easterners were met by Rome's middlemen, the Greeks of southern Italy, who paid in cash, wine and olive oil for the luxuries the Romans wanted.

Trouble then came from an unexpected quarter. For years, Rhodes' navy had policed the eastern Mediterranean and kept it free from pirates. Now that navy was in decline—but Rome had no interest in assuming its policing role. Indeed, pirates provided a welcome source of slaves for Rome's western markets. The unhindered corsairs multiplied. Those of Cilicia, on the rugged southern coast of Asia Minor, virtually formed a pirate nation, with a fleet of 1,000 ships.

The pirates cruised at will through the eastern Mediterranean, and soon extended their range westward to infest even the shores of Italy. They forced protection money from coastal cities, and kidnapped Roman noblewomen within a few miles of the capital, holding them for ransom. Two government dignitaries were abducted, along with their staffs. A consular flotilla was attacked while at anchor in Rome's port of Ostia. Only when pirates overran Delos and sacked the port in 69 B.C. did Rome at last respond.

In 67 B.C. the People's Assembly turned to a skilled administrator named Pompey, directing him to use whatever force he considered necessary to wipe out piracy throughout the Mediterranean. Pompey proceeded on a mammoth campaign. He requisitioned ships from every province and tributary nation, creating separate fleets under separate leaders, and ordered a simultaneous attack on pirate bases all over the sea (page 114-115). His master plan worked: The Mediterranean was swept clean from west to east. Pompey did not execute all of the pirates, but settled the most promising as farmers in the hinterlands of the Roman world, thereby removing the temptation for them to resume their campaign of harassment.

But now Rome was beset by danger from within. For a period of almost three decades after Pompey cleared the sea of pirates, the Republic was wracked by civil strife. First, Pompey and Julius Caesar battled for dominance. Both died at the hands of assassins. Then Caesar's grand-nephew Octavian, combining guile and force, liquidated one after another would-be successor to Caesar—all but the veteran general, Mark Antony. The two survivors formed a wary alliance, dividing Rome's territorial possessions between them, with Octavian taking Italy and the West and Antony laying claim to the East, where he joined forces with Cleopatra, the Queen of Egypt. But Octavian, true to the spirit of his great-uncle, wanted it all. So the stage was set for the last of the great Roman civil wars—a conflict decided finally not by armies, but by two titanic fleets of galleys whose clashes spelled the end of one era and the dawn of another.

Antony was a soldier's soldier, rough, high-living, blustery, zestful—as much a splendid animal as a man. His bullish good looks were typically Roman, and he modeled himself on the swaggering comportment of Hercules—the Romans' name for the Greek demigod Herakles—whom he fancifully claimed as an ancestor. These qualities offended the historian Plutarch, who wrote of Antony's "boastfulness, his drinking horn in evidence, his sitting by a comrade who was eating, or his standing to eat at a soldier's table—it is astonishing how much goodwill and affection for him all this produced in his soldiers." By the time his hour of confrontation with Octavian approached, Antony was in his fifties and his powers were declining, sapped not only by wine and war, but also by the luxury-loving court of Cleopatra, whom he married in 37 B.C.

Compared to Cleopatra, Antony was a child. He came from the masculine ambiance of the Roman West. She belonged, heart and mind, to the Hellenistic East—a world old in subtlety, luxurious, ceremonial, shot through with a dark sophistication. Like the rest of the Ptolemies, she was not a native Egyptian, but a Greek, and was the fruit of generations of inbreeding—for the Ptolemaic kings married within the family, occasionally even wedding their sisters. Highly intelligent and deeply ambitious, she schemed to gain from Rome all the traditional lands of her royal ancestors.

Octavian was every bit her match in wiliness. In 32 B.C. he appeared before the Roman Senate and read a document that he claimed was Mark Antony's will: It bequeathed to Cleopatra all of the Roman East. As Octavian had anticipated, the Senators were outraged. They empowered him to strip Antony of his command and to declare war on Cleopatra. The showdown came only months later.

In 31 B.C. Antony and Cleopatra, with a fleet of 500 warships and 300 merchantmen, and an army of some 75,000 Roman legionnaires, 12,000 cavalrymen and 25,000 light-armed infantrymen, hovered on a front that stretched down the whole western shore of Greece. Octavian and his veteran general Marcus Vipsanius Agrippa concentrated their

Pompey: the pirates' nemesis

By the First Century B.C., pirates were rampaging throughout the Mediterranean world, not only preying on merchantmen but also descending on coastal towns to gather human booty for the slave trade. Occasionally the brigands overstepped themselves.

Such was the case with a band of sea rovers that kidnapped young Julius Caesar as he was traveling to Rhodes to study law. When they asked a ransom, Caesar's friends paid up—and Caesar promptly raised a squadron of warships, captured his captors and crucified them, as he had told them he would.

In 67 B.C. the Roman Senate entrusted the job of eliminating the pirate menace to the veteran soldier Pompey, supplying him with 120,000 men and 270 warships. Pompey divided the Mediterranean and Black Seas into sectors (right), assigned a commander to each and ordered them to attack simultaneously, early in the spring. With Pompey's 60-ship fleet leading the roundup, the Roman forces subdued the corsairs in their hideouts or drove them eastward to Cilicia, in Asia Minor, where the remnants were captured. In a matter of months, the pirate plague had been eradicated.

To rid the Mediterranean world of the threat of piracy, Pompey (right) coordinated attacks in 13 areas, leaving Cilicia untouched. The pirates who fled there were then rounded up en masse.

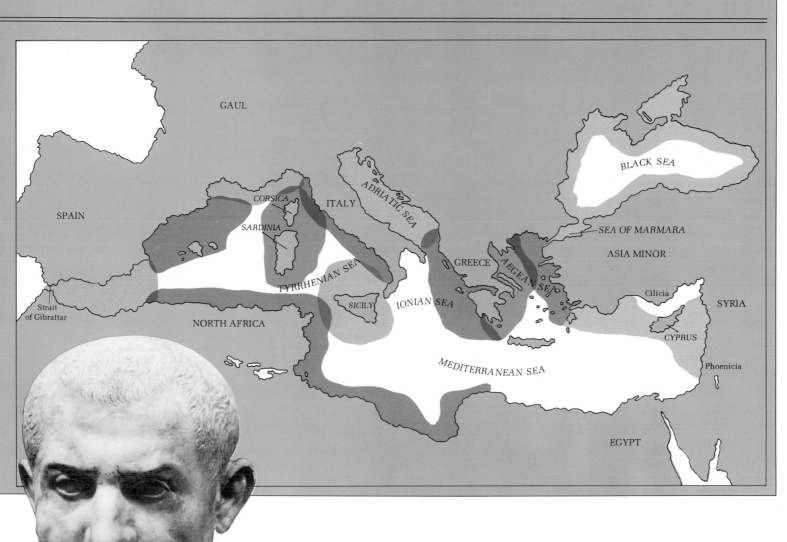

forces in the southern Italian ports of Brundisium and Tarentum—400 ships and a tightly knit Roman army of about 80,000 foot soldiers and 12,000 cavalrymen.

Although Octavian had seen naval action, he was never happy in war; he preferred the quieter ruthlessness of politics. But in entrusting his fortunes in battle to Agrippa, he had made a typically astute move. At the age of 32, this general was a man of huge military talents and unfaltering loyalty. Agrippa seemed the paragon of his age: abstemious in his habits, widely cultivated and morally irreproachable. Even the gossiping Roman annalists could leave no stain on him. And he demonstrated his brilliance from the start.

While Antony and Cleopatra, surrounded by their vast fleet, lay in wait at the Greek port of Patras near the entrance to the Gulf of Corinth, Agrippa outflanked them. Despite the unpredictable weather of early March of 31 B.C., he crossed the sea by an unfrequented route and fell upon Antony's base at Methone on the southwest tip of Greece. This powerful outpost was taken by surprise and captured, and from there

Agrippa began to harass the grain ships that were bringing up supplies to Antony from Egypt. It was an inspired opening move, and one that would cost Antony dearly.

Next, Agrippa raided Antony's bases to the north and so diverted attention from his real thrust: the transport of Octavian's troops across the sea from Italy. This was accomplished with speed and secrecy, and by the end of March the invading fleet and army lay only 30 miles to the north of Antony's headquarters in the Ambracian Gulf.

Octavian, arriving to join the battle, now waited. The great sheltered gulf was all but impregnable by sea, for its mouth was closed by straits less than half a mile wide. And on either side of the narrows, Antony's men had constructed forts whose giant catapults could deluge passing ships with stones and fire. But in fortifying himself, Antony had also trapped himself, and Cleopatra as well. For the initiative lay with Octavian and Agrippa. Antony's main fleet was blockaded in its harbor. And now Octavian threatened Antony's army too, by marching an imposing force of his own to the 400-foot hill of Mikhalitzi, overlooking the bay from the northwest.

Antony and Cleopatra, hurrying to the Ambracian Gulf from Patras, found their navies split. Many of their ships were trapped inside the gulf, and the rest were scattered in harbors along the coast. Meanwhile, Agrippa detached some of Octavian's fleet to mop up these isolated squadrons. One by one Antony's other bases, including Patras, lost their protective ships and were occupied by Octavian's troops.

While the enemy waited confidently outside the gulf, summer began to take its toll on Antony's men. Disease—probably malaria and dysentery—spread through the tents, especially in the encampment on the southern point of the constricted and unhealthy headland of Actium. Deaths led to desertions. To replace those lost, Antony had to send soldiers inland to kidnap farmers, muleteers and vagrants. Supplies ran critically low; a few blockade runners slipped through the enemy squadrons, but not enough to feed Antony's increasingly restive and mutinous men. Even many of his officers began deserting to join Octavian's forces, some because they were convinced their cause was lost, others because they heartily disliked Cleopatra.

On a misty morning in early August, Antony's fleet made a sudden move to break out. Admiral Gaius Sosius, one of his most trusted and experienced supporters, pushed through the straits in swirling fog and routed a blockading squadron. One moment it seemed as if the situation was saved. The next, Agrippa had sailed up with the rest of the fleet and had pushed Sosius back.

The waiting game resumed. Through the month of August, Antony's fleet lay at its moorings and his soldiers fretted with inaction. By the end of August, his fleet and army had been under siege for four months. Antony summoned his generals and admirals to the southern promontory of Actium, and called a council of war. He had only two choices left. He could abandon his fleet and march eastward into Greece; or he could embark the cream of his soldiers and attempt to break out, leaving the rest of his army to fend for itself.

Lucius Canidius Crassus, his land commander, argued for withdrawing into Greece and for deciding the issue in battle there. An action by sea would divide and fritter the army's strength, he pointed out. All of Antony's past successes had been won on land.

Cleopatra, on the other hand, argued for a forceful naval action, emphasizing the difficulties of an overland retreat through the mountains of Macedonia. Even then they would be cut off from Egypt by Octavian's galleys. Moreover, Cleopatra could not leave her fleet behind; in the hold of her flagship was most of Egypt's treasure. Nor could she attempt a breakout alone.

Antony acceded to her case. He realized that, without a fleet, his army would be all but cut off by the enemy from escape farther east. But if the flower of the troops and the navy could be extricated from the snare at Actium, then Antony might fall back on the rich and populous provinces of Cyrenaica and Syria (where he still had seven legions) and gather strength for another day.

So whether because of strategy or love, Antony and Cleopatra decided to face their fate together rather than separately. The circling shores of Ambracia—once a haven, now a trap—had thinned out Antony's soldiers and his oarsmen, but evidently not his infatuation.

The forces that faced each other were unequal. Antony's remnant of sailors and oarsmen was insufficient to man his whole fleet. So he burned the smaller warships and many merchantmen. Of the 230 vessels left to him, most were larger than those of Octavian—high-built galleys that ranged from ordinary triremes up to monstrous tenners. At the water line, their flanks were girded with massive, ironbound timbers as protection against ramming; and the heavy towers fore and aft were filled by Antony with archers and slingers.

He divided the fleet into four squadrons. Cleopatra's force was a flotilla of 60, including some merchantmen. The other three squadrons carried the bulk of the fighting men, embarked from camps overlooking the bay. They included 20,000 selected legionnaires and 2,000 archers—all battle-tested veterans. But they were used to following Antony on land. Plutarch described one grizzled officer, his body covered with battle scars, calling out to Antony in disgust as he was being embarked: "Imperator, why do you distrust these wounds and this sword and put your hopes in miserable logs of wood? Let Egyptians and Phoenicians do their fighting at sea, but give us land, on which we are accustomed to stand and either conquer our enemies or die." To this, Plutarch added, "Antony made no reply."

Against these juggernauts, poised to bludgeon their way to freedom, Octavian opposed 400 war galleys. Lighter and lower than those of the enemy, but equipped like them with turrets and reinforcing belts of timbers, they ranged in size from biremes to sixers. Among them were several examples of the *liburnian*—a light, fast, two-banked galley adapted from vessels used by the Liburnians, pirates of the Adriatic. On these ships Octavian embarked eight and a half legions— some 40,000 men, almost twice the force of Antony. They were Italian legionnaires, loyal and finely disciplined. Their ships were equipped less for ramming than for boarding, and they carried an added weapon, perfected by Agrippa. This was a heavy grapnel fired at long range from a catapult on the deck. Once it had fallen across an enemy bulwark, it was harder to hack away than a conventional grappling device, for its head consisted of a sharp steel pole that embedded itself in the deck like the iron spike of the raven. Octavian's ships, though perhaps not faster than Antony's, were more maneuverable. Their decks were stripped for action, and—as was customary in battle—they were driven only by oarsmen. Antony's ships revealingly carried their sails stacked on deck, portending flight.

On August 29, as Antony's fleet was preparing to move out, a storm swept along the coast. For four days mountainous seas pounded the shore and roared through the gulf's narrow passage. Agrippa took his fleet behind a headland to ride it out, and Antony's ships rocked gently inside the protected bay. Ashore, 50,000 soldiers huddled in their billowing tents. Antony had left them under the command of Canidius Crassus, with instructions to march inland and make for Asia Minor overland as soon as the fleet had escaped. Encamped on their storm-wracked strand beside the skeletons of burned-out ships, they must have known they were being sacrificed.

The storm faded and the morning of September 2 dawned clear. Beyond the harbor mouth, where the sea spread in a sparkling plane of blue, Octavian's galleys were already mustering. Octavian had gone ashore to wait out the storm, knowing that the seas had been running too high for Antony to venture out. On this morning of the battle, he left his tent before sunrise to review the fleet. According to the historian Dio Cassius, the general addressed his embarking soldiers, pouring scorn on the enemy—"Alexandrians and Egyptians . . . who worship reptiles and beasts as gods, who embalm their own bodies to give them the semblance of immortality, who are most reckless in effrontery but most feeble in courage, and who, worst of all, are slaves to a woman and not to a man."

Antony, meanwhile, was aware that three months on hard rations had wasted his men body and soul. So he sought to steel them and reassure them by stressing the might of their ships. "For you yourselves, of course," he said, "see the length and beam of our vessels, which are such that even if the enemy's were a match for them in number, yet because of these advantages on our side they could do no damage either by charging bows on or by ramming our sides. For in the one case the thickness of our timbers, and in the other the very height of our ships, would certainly check them, even if there were no one on board to ward them off."

Now, in the translucent dawn, the vessels of Antony and Cleopatra came filing through the straits of the Ambracian Gulf into the open sea. On the mainland the camps of both Octavian and Antony, stripped of their best fighting men, watched the scene without moving against each other. Antony's four squadrons crossed the shallow harbor bar and spread out in two ranks on a front one and a half miles long. Then, with its wings still protected from Octavian's greater numbers by the retreating headlands to either side, Antony's fleet came to a halt. In the right-hand squadron sailed Antony and his second admiral, Gellius Publicola; with the left went Gaius Sosius. And behind the center hovered Cleopatra's squadron of 60 vessels, ready to seize a chance of flight

The fatal allure of Egypt's Queen

A bust of Octavian flatters him by emphasizing his eyes, which he believed could dazzle the people about him.

The seeds of the Battle of Actium were sown in the Roman Senate on the Ides of March, 44 B.C., when Julius Caesar was assassinated. His designated heir, Octavian (*above*), Caesar's grand-nephew and adopted son, found it necessary at first to form a series of expedient alliances with other contenders for Caesar's mantle, especially Mark Antony (*far right*). Together Octavian and Antony disposed of others and divided the empire; Octavian ruled in the west and Antony in the east. But any hope of stability was soon destroyed by Egypt's queen—a woman of mesmerizing appeal and boundless ambition.

Cleopatra VII had schemed for greater empire since the time of Caesar, in the process becoming Caesar's mistress and bearing a son she said was his. Now she turned her blandishments on Antony. From the time she paid a royal visit to the veteran commander at his headquarters in Cilicia—theatrically arriving in a golden-canopied, purple-sailed barge—Cleopatra held him in thrall. An outbreak of war in the west forced Antony to return to Rome, where he tried to strengthen the fragile bond with Octavian by marrying his sister Octavia. But on his return east Antony succumbed again and abandoned Octavia for Cleopatra. With the unwelcome alliance finally broken, Octavian crushed Antony and Cleopatra at Actium, hounded them until they found release in suicide, then returned to Rome in triumph, to be crowned Emperor Augustus.

The tangled drama of these three was not yet played out, however. Cleopatra had had two sons by Antony. Augustus permitted them to come to Rome, where he made sure that they remained powerless to challenge his new dynasty. Toward the young man who Cleopa-

tra asserted was Julius Caesar's offspring, he was not so benign. Cleopatra had named her son Caesarion and had designated him Ptolemy XIV, her co-ruler and successor to Egypt's throne. Now, of course, Egypt belonged to Rome, and thus to Augustus. But the thought that a possible son of Caesar's was lurking in the wings troubled the Emperor. Augustus settled matters with characteristic decisiveness: He saw to it that Caesarion-Ptolemy XIV was assassinated.

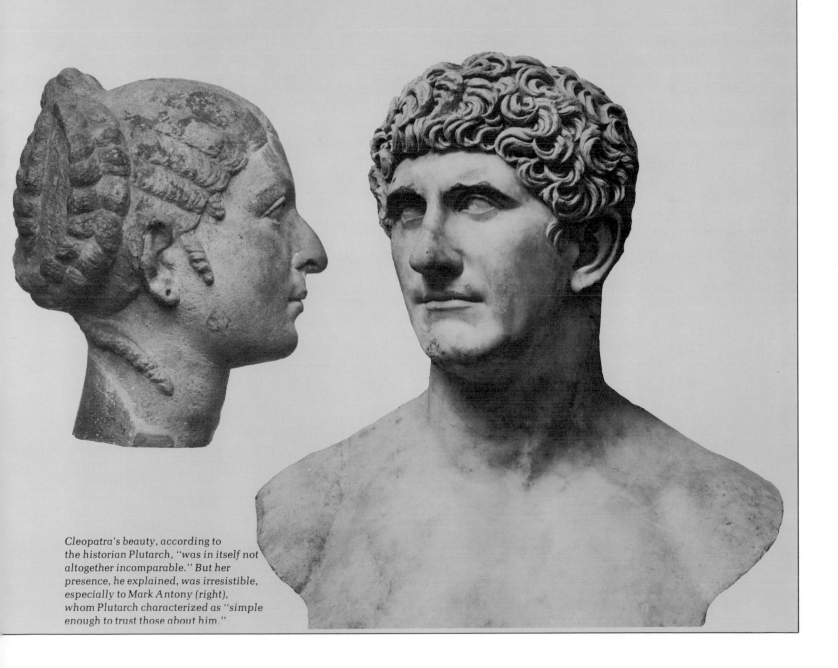

Cleopatra's beauty, according to the historian Plutarch, "was in itself not altogether incomparable." But her presence, he explained, was irresistible, especially to Mark Antony (right), whom Plutarch characterized as "simple enough to trust those about him."

*More histrionic than the Battle of
Actium itself, this 17th Century painting
depicts warships clashing while a
plump Cleopatra languorously looks on
from a royal barge (left). The artist
dressed the sailors and marines in the
costumes of his own age, gave them
Viking-like shields, and placed them
aboard vessels bearing decorations
and rigging unknown to the Romans.*

through the heart of the opposing lines. The Queen herself was carried by her flagship *Antonias*, on which she kept a hoard of gold, silver coin and bars, and jewels.

Antony's strategy was to take his stand at the entrance to the gulf, and make Octavian's fleet come to him. So the two fleets watched each other until noon, with a mile of calm sea between them. At their benches under the decks, stifling in the September heat, the rowers leaned apprehensively on their oars. Above them, under the burning sun, the soldiers sweated in armored ranks.

When he saw that the enemy was not going to advance, Antony tried one last gamble; it depended on a local phenomenon of which he was aware and perhaps the men from Rome were not. Usually, in this part of Greece, a breeze sprang up from the west at midday, veered into the northwest and freshened into a healthy wind. With such a wind, if it was strong enough, Antony could loose his sails, outstrip Agrippa's oarsmen, round the island of Leukas southwest of them and save most of his fleet—not by battle but by flight.

Indeed Plutarch reported, shortly, "a wind was rising from the sea." Whipping the surface into small whitecaps, it first came from the west, almost head on; so Antony could not yet raise his sails. He would have to depend upon his oarsmen to gain the sea room necessary to round the headland to the south. And now he gave the signal to advance.

His admiral Sosius, on the left wing and farther south, led the way. Octavian, on the flank facing Sosius, backed water to lure him farther out. Agrippa, facing Antony and Publicola, immediately extended his line to envelop Antony's wing. Both protagonists were now maneuvering for sea room—Antony to escape and Agrippa and Octavian to outflank him by covering his fleet in a wide crescent.

But Octavian's fleet did not retreat far enough west for Antony's purposes. To clear the cape south of him, he needed even more sea room. And the wind still held from the west. He could not avoid direct combat. So he sent his forward lines against the enemy.

A storm of stones and flaming missiles whirred from the ships' catapults on either side. Lodged high in their wooden turrets, the stone-throwing engines of Antony's hefty ships were especially formidable. They filled the air and spattered the sea and ships with a variety of projectiles: boulders, giant arrows, flaming hemp.

These heavy ships, thrusting forward, at last reached the enemy. Crammed with their soldiers and engines of war, their cumbersome sails still stowed on deck and their sides heavy with reinforced wood, they pushed sluggishly into the opposing fleet. Agrippa had kept his line two deep to receive them, and he absorbed the charge with a buffer of lighter galleys. Each of Antony's warships was assailed by two or three opponents charging from different angles. Agrippa's galleys, more maneuverable, wove in and out, ramming and retiring, then returning to ram again, or speeding in close and shattering banks of oars. Antony's monsters attempted to grapple and hold them, or to overwhelm them with catapult fire. Sometimes, when ships became locked together, Antony's veterans swept the opposing decks or showered them with stones from above. In their turrets, the slingers and archers poured a terrible fire

One of the many mementos of the Battle of Actium was this imperial medal struck after Octavian's victory. One side awards equal credit to Agrippa by placing the general (left) alongside Octavian; the other features a crocodile chained to a palm branch, denoting the defeat of Egypt's Queen Cleopatra.

on the legionnaires, locked in hand-to-hand combat below them. At other times Agrippa's swift ramming tactics sank the enemy, for all their massive belts of timber.

But Plutarch writes that often Agrippa's galleys did not dare engage Antony's head on, because of their colossal prows and rams. So the fight eventually stagnated into clusters of ships locked together, Antony's men defending, while Agrippa's warriors hacked at the tower-like hulks of the enemy ships with pikes and firebrands.

It was inevitable that Antony's smaller fleet should eventually be surrounded, and he must have known this. Rather than be outflanked, he and Publicola moved their right-hand squadron outward to face Agrippa's swarms. Pushing ever west and north, they also increased their chance of clearing Leukas island to the south and making good their flight. Soon they had broken with their center altogether. A gap opened and slowly widened.

Finally, between two and three in the afternoon, the freshening wind veered into the north. And Cleopatra made her move.

Her flagship *Antonias* was seen to shake out its great purple sails and lurch forward. With her squadron of 60 galleys and merchantmen following her, Cleopatra swiftly sailed straight through the center gap. The *Antonias* reached the open ocean and turned south for Egypt. Not only the Queen's own galleys, but as many of those in the battle as could break free turned to follow her, hoisting their sails and toppling their catapults, grapnels, and even some of their fortified turrets into the sea to lighten the ships and hasten their speed. But among those too tightly locked in combat to join the flight was Antony's flagship.

Calling for a fast quinquereme, however, he hastened after Cleopatra; "he was swayed by the sentiments neither of a commander nor of a brave man," Plutarch lamented. "He forgot everything else, betrayed and ran away from those who were fighting and dying in his cause . . . and hastened after the woman who had already ruined him and would make his ruin still more complete."

Antony's captains were surrounded by the mass of Agrippa's galleys, and few were able to follow their commander. In particular, the left wing under Sosius, hemmed in against Leukas, had no hope of escape. But for a while they fought on. Agrippa's men, wrote Dio Cassius, "damaged the lower parts of the ships all around, crushed the oars, snapped off the rudders, and climbing on the decks, seized hold of some of the foe and pulled them down, pushed off others, and fought with yet others." For their part, "Antony's men pushed their assailants back with boat hooks, cut them down with axes, hurled down upon them stones and heavy missiles."

Antony and Cleopatra meanwhile were in full flight southward. Antony's quinquereme caught up with Cleopatra, and she signaled him to come on board. But he could not face her. "Instead," wrote Plutarch, "he went forward alone to the prow and sat down by himself in silence, holding his head in both hands."

Agrippa's heavier-oared ships, without their sails aboard, could not overtake Antony. But several swift *liburnians* took up the chase. As they came up with the *Antonias*, Antony took command of the flagship and turned her to face them. All of the *liburnians* shied away from the powerful flagship, except one, commanded by a Spartan named Eurycles. Years earlier, Antony had beheaded Eurycles' father for robbery, and the Spartan now shook his lance at Antony from his deck.

Antony shouted at him from the poop of the *Antonias*. "Who is this that pursues Antony?"

"I am Eurycles the son of Lachares," the man shouted back, "whom the fortune of Caesar enables to avenge the death of his father."

Eurycles sent his galley plunging at the *Antonias*. But the flagship's well-trained oarsmen swept her out of the attacker's path, and Eurycles' vessel smashed into another ship, spinning her around. Bouncing off this galley, he came alongside another and grappled with it. This one turned out to contain Antony's plate and furniture, which Eurycles seized. In the meantime the *Antonias* escaped.

To the north Antony's fleet was gradually being worn down. Hopelessly outnumbered, abandoned by their leader, many captains and crews surrendered. Others fled or were blown back into the gulf, where they faced another blockade until they too capitulated.

But still others, wrote Dio Cassius, battled on into the dusk. Many of these were probably the great sixers, seveners and eighters beloved of the eastern Mediterranean fleets. Floating castles, they resisted all attack, until Agrippa decided to resort to the ultimate weapon of fire.

Flaming projectiles were catapulted onto the big ships' decks, along with pots of charcoal and burning pitch. Aboard other galleys, the legionnaires threw javelins with torches at their tips. At first the defenders doused the fires with their drinking water, then with sea water hauled up in buckets. But the wind-fanned flames spread across the wooden decks and ignited the rowing benches. Desperately, the men tried to smother them with their heavy cloaks, and even with corpses. "But later," wrote Dio Cassius, "especially when the wind raged furiously, the flames flared up more than ever, fed by this very fuel. So long as only a part of a ship was on fire, men would stand by that part and leap into it, hewing away or scattering the timbers; and these detached timbers were hurled by some into the sea and by others against their opponents."

Some galleys moved to grapple with Agrippa's ships, in the hope of burning them or of boarding and saving themselves. But the enemy stood off. Soon the great galleys had become giant infernos. Many of the sailors were suffocated by the smoke, while the oarsmen perished in the roaring flames. Soldiers tried to strip off their armor—and were pierced by arrows from Agrippa's galleys. Others were roasted to death, or threw themselves into the sea and drowned trying to swim to shore. Still others committed suicide.

By nighttime the battle was over, and only a few charred hulks glimmered fitfully on the heaving sea. Some 130 of Antony's ships had fallen into Agrippa's hands, and 30 or 40 more were sunk. The casualties among Antony's troops probably numbered little more than 5,000, for the size of their ships had saved many of them until the point of surrender; the casualties among the crews are unknown—but they were far greater. Of Agrippa's losses, the historians are silent. Certainly they were less than Antony's.

A cunning course to power

For all its apocalyptic fury, the Battle of Actium in 31 B.C. was a shrewdly planned last move in a power game that Octavian had been playing for 13 years. His route to dominance was, in fact, nothing less than a masterpiece of military and political maneuvering, and it has inspired frequent artistic homage ever since. Here and on the following three pages, for example, his rise is dramatized in spectacular Flemish tapestries created in the 16th Century.

The struggle began in 44 B.C. when his great-uncle Julius Caesar—the strong man of the empire—was assassinated. Though Caesar's will named 18-year-old Octavian his heir, the youth's claim to office seemed extremely precarious. Caesar's killers had fled to Greece to gather strength for a campaign to win control of the empire. At home, two of Caesar's lieutenants, Mark Antony and another soldier named Lepidus, sought the mantle of their dead leader. To further complicate matters, a fifth rival, Pompey's son Sextus, had taken command of much of Rome's navy.

Faced with enemies on every side, Octavian adopted a carefully staged strategy. His first military move was to attack Antony, defeating him at Mutina, in northern Italy. He then shrewdly formed an alliance with both Antony and Lepidus, promising to share rule of the empire with them in return for their help in defeating Caesar's assassins. Together, they routed Brutus and Cassius at Philippi, in northern Greece.

Still playing for time, Octavian kept his word and awarded the East to Antony, Africa to Lepidus and took the West for himself. Next, with revenues generated by heavy taxes, he bought or built 370 warships, which he used to defeat the navy of Sextus off Sicily in 36 B.C. Thus strengthened, he reclaimed the African provinces from Lepidus; and five years later he was ready to take the final, inevitable step: Mark Antony, his first victim, became his last.

Rome and all its dominions were now his, and Octavian gave himself a title worthy of his position—Augustus, or "Revered One." The scheming warrior thereupon became a benevolent dictator, renouncing war and laying the foundation of a peaceful prosperity that would endure for more than three centuries.

Unwittingly serving the schemes of Octavian for total power, a bareheaded Antony leads a successful attack on the forces of Caesar's assassins at Philippi in 42 B.C. After they were defeated, both Cassius and Brutus committed suicide.

As Cleopatra prepares to flee from the scene of the Battle of Actium in her galley (right), Antony (left), realizing their combined fleet faces defeat by Octavian's navy, rushes to join her. Within a year they had committed suicide in Egypt, ending the civil wars that had plagued Rome for more than a century.

Returning from Egypt, Octavian enters Rome in triumph
in *29 B.C.* In his left hand he holds a scepter symbolizing his new
power as sole consul of the Empire, while a general carries
his crown. Two years later he was named Emperor by the Senate.

To Octavian and Agrippa at the time, their victory cannot have seemed complete. Whatever the cost to them in men and ships, Antony and Cleopatra had escaped with about a third of their fleet and with their treasury intact: Soon they would be in Egypt preparing to resume the war. But at home, the Battle of Actium was seen to mark the border between the days of the Roman Republic and the days of the Empire. For the Romans of the West it became the battle par excellence—the moment that liberated them from the threat of the decadent, Hellenistic East, from the sorceress of Egypt.

Cleopatra continued in Roman propaganda as an Egyptian whore-queen, sensual and degenerate. She had abandoned battle, it was declared, not as part of a tactical plan, but because of personal cowardice, and had thus betrayed her infatuated lover, who fled after her.

The other Roman imperial legend—that Actium was a decisive battle—is more accurate. Antony and Cleopatra never recovered from it. Soon afterward, the army of Canidius Crassus negotiated its own surrender, and Octavian's troops were established in Greece. Then the legions of Asia Minor and Syria turned against Antony, and he was left to face the might of Rome with the support only of Egypt, still loyal to its Queen.

Antony, closeted in his seaside villa, fell into fatalistic gloom. Cleopatra, more resilient, hatched an extravagant scheme of recovery: They would escape to India or the Arabian Sea, she decided, and she had ships hauled from the Nile to the Red Sea for the purpose. But the flotilla no sooner had been carried laboriously overland when it was seized and burned by a local Arab king.

In the summer of 30 B.C., Octavian marched on Egypt from Syria. Antony, with a pitifully inferior fleet and army, faced him in the suburbs of Alexandria. But Antony's cavalry deserted, his infantry were crushed, and the fleet surrendered without a blow. Antony, informed that Cleopatra had committed suicide, fell on his sword. But as he lay dying he heard that she was alive, and he asked to be taken to her. The Queen had walled herself into her own prepared mausoleum, together with the choicest objects of her treasury and a mass of firewood. The mausoleum's door was locked from the inside. So she and her two serving women hauled Antony up by ropes through an aperture in the top, and he died in her arms.

When Octavian's forces entered the heart of the city, Cleopatra tried to negotiate. But Octavian's troops broke into her mausoleum before she could set fire to her treasury. Later, afraid that Octavian intended to lead her in his triumphal parade through Rome, she decided to kill herself, and wrote a letter to him, asking that she be buried beside Antony. Octavian sent his men rushing to her palace. They arrived to find her lying in her state robes on a golden couch. She was already dead, probably from the bite of an asp, sacred symbol of the Pharaohs. Her serving maids, Iras and Charmian, lay dying at her feet. Cleopatra's manner of death, said Charmian, was "befitting the descendant of so many kings."

It was the epitaph of the whole Hellenistic world, which perished at the Battle of Actium. Thereafter, for more than 200 years, the Mediterranean was to become a Roman lake: rich, united and at peace.

Pax Romana in a sea-centered Empire

wo letters written by seamen during the Second or Third Century A.D. speak of the maritime age that followed the Battle of Actium. They are mundane documents, but their placid, positive tone takes the measure of a whole era. This was a time of prosperity and optimism, when the stability of the Roman Empire turned the Mediterranean into, for Romans, Mare Nostrum—"Our Sea."

The first letter was written by a crew member on a grain ship that had arrived at Portus, downriver from Rome.

"Dear Apollinarius:

"Many greetings. I pray continuously for your health; I am well. I'm writing to let you know that I reached land on June 30 and that we unloaded on July 12. I went up to Rome on the 19th and the place welcomed us as the god wished. We are daily expecting our sailing orders; up to today not one of the grain fleet has been released. Best regards to your wife, and Serenus, and all your friends. Goodbye.

"Your brother Irenaeus"

The writer of the second letter, an Egyptian youth, had enlisted in the Roman navy and had been assigned to Rome's crack fleet, which was based at Misenum, near Naples.

"Dear Father:

"First of all, I hope you are well and will always be well, and my sister and her daughter and my brother. I thank the god Serapis that when I was in danger on the sea he quickly came to the rescue. When I arrived at Misenum I received from the government three gold pieces for my traveling expenses. I'm fine. Please write me, Father, first to tell me that you are well, second that my sister and brother are well, and third so that I can kiss your hand because you gave me a good education, and because of it I hope to get quick promotion if the gods are willing."

The young man's name was Apion. He had every reason to expect an agreeable career, for by the Second Century A.D. the Roman navy functioned less as an active fighting force than as a deterrent. It guarded harbors and trade routes, supplied the army, and carried dispatches and government personnel.

In 29 B.C. Octavian had become Augustus Caesar, Rome's first Emperor. One of his major achievements had been to organize the navy in a mold so effective that his successors barely changed it for two centuries. As Pompey had done when fighting pirates, Octavian divided the sea into sectors and assigned squadrons to patrol them. By the end of the First Century A.D., naval protection had been extended along the Dan-

In a plaque carved in the Third Century A.D., a merchantman glides into the man-made harbor of Portus, near Rome. As the crew prepares to tie up at a wharf, the vessel's owner, his wife and the captain stand on the high stern. A statue of Neptune (right foreground) dominates a jetty, and the lighthouse (background) is crowned by a flaming beacon.

ube and the coast of the Black Sea in the northeast and, in the northwest, to Britain and the frontiers of Germany, where a squadron patrolled the Rhine. The eastern Mediterranean was guarded by Roman fleets stationed in Alexandria and Syria, and the Adriatic by a fleet based at Ravenna, on the east coast of Italy.

But the heart of Roman naval operations became Misenum. From this base—consisting of a well-sheltered inner harbor connected by a narrow channel to an outer harbor that was actually a half-sunken volcanic crater—the state fleet par excellence maintained a patrol of the western Mediterranean and supervised the rest of it. The Prefect of Misenum was the most powerful man in the navy—so powerful that the post was given not to an officer of the navy but to a trusted functionary of the imperial administration.

While most of the provincial squadrons were made up of light galleys and liburnians, the 50-ship fleet that was based at Misenum consisted chiefly of triremes or still heavier vessels—quadriremes, quinqueremes and a sixer flagship. These warships were little different from those of earlier years, apart from such innovations as a fighting tower in the bow and a commander's cabin aft. The vessels' names—*Clementia*, *Pax*, *Justitia*, *Pietas*, *Providentia* were favorites—reflected the stability and order of the Empire.

The crews and marines of the Roman navy were not native Romans, for something of the old landlubber's antipathy to the sea still ran strong. The Romans seemed to look at the sea as if from the beach: The water was a place by which to own a villa. *"O happy man, he doesn't know what perils / He's escaped, who's never put to sea."* So wrote the playwright Terence, and he meant it.

His view was shared by the First Century Emperor Domitian, who insisted on making any sea journey in a dinghy that was towed well behind a galley: The sound of a galley's oars, he said, shattered his nerves. Romans were fond of fishing as a pastime, but this was no anomaly; most such fishing could be done from the shore. The poet Martial described one villa that was comfortably arranged so one could fish not merely from the bedroom window but even from the bed.

The sailors in the imperial Roman fleets were the traditional seafaring peoples of the Mediterranean: Greeks, Syrians, Phoenicians, Egyptians, even the river-loving Slavs. Between the ages of 18 and 23, countless youths from obscure parts of the Empire—Balkan villages, Middle Eastern ports, Aegean islets—made their way to the great naval centers of Misenum and Ravenna and enlisted there. Until 160 A.D., marriage was forbidden to them, as it was to soldiers (being thought incompatible with active service). Sailors set up homes with local women or took slaves as concubines, but their children could legally assume only their mother's name. After 26 to 28 years of service, they were rewarded with Roman citizenship, and when death claimed them, they were buried at Misenum or Ravenna beneath proud little tombstones commemorating their careers.

Among Romans, the navy was always less respected than the army. However, its appeal to the old maritime nations seems to have been great. "I have learned from Tilis," wrote an Egyptian named Sempronius

to his son in Alexandria, "that, yielding to his persuasion, you have not enlisted in the fleet, and I have spent two days grieving. Henceforth see to it that you are not persuaded, else you will no longer be my son. You know that you differ from and surpass your brothers in everything easily. You will do well to enter a fine service."

The navy may have lacked the glamor of the legions—indeed, enlistment in the army was open only to Roman citizens until the Third Century A.D., when additional manpower was needed—but the navy's recruiting and training procedures were much like those used by the army. A youth swore an oath of allegiance to the Emperor and was hustled off to training camp. There he built up his strength with physical drills and was taught to handle arms.

Warship crews, whatever the size, were divided into the army's

The tombstone of a Roman shipwright of the Second Century A.D., Publius Longidienus, shows him at his labors. The inscription at top proudly announces that the monument was partly paid for by P. Longidienus Rufio and P. Longidienus Philadespotus—grateful slaves set free by their late shipwright master.

The prodigious riches of Rome's dominions

BALTIC SEA

BRITAIN

GERMANY

Rutupiae

Gesoriacum

GAUL

Olbia

Marseilles

Aquileia

Tomi

Narbonne

SPAIN

Luna

Forum Julii

ITALY

Ancona

Corsica

Centum
Cellae · Rome

Tarraco

Dyrrachium

Byzantium

Sardinia

Portus

Thrace

Gades

Pozzuoli

Tarentum

Macedonia

Carthago Nova

Brundisium

Caesarea

Messina

Ephesus

Lilybaeum

Sicily

GREECE

Athens

Miletus

Carthage

Syracuse

Rhodes

Hadrumetum

Crete

MEDITERRANEAN SEA

NORTH AFRICA

Sabratha   Leptis Magna

Apollonia

Alexandria

EGYPT

▼ Amber	Grain	◢ Marble	Silphium
◆ Brass	⬢ Hides	Myrrh	■ Silver
● Copper	Honey	◓ Olive Oil	Spices
◉ Fish	▢ Horses	Papyrus	Textiles
Flax	◖ Iron	Parchment	◇ Timber
◣ Frankincense	◗ Ivory	Pottery	◗ Tin
Fruit	▲ Lead	Purple Dye	◖ Wild Beasts
◑ Glass	◆ Leather Goods	◣ Salt	Wine
◖ Gold	Linen	Silk	Wool

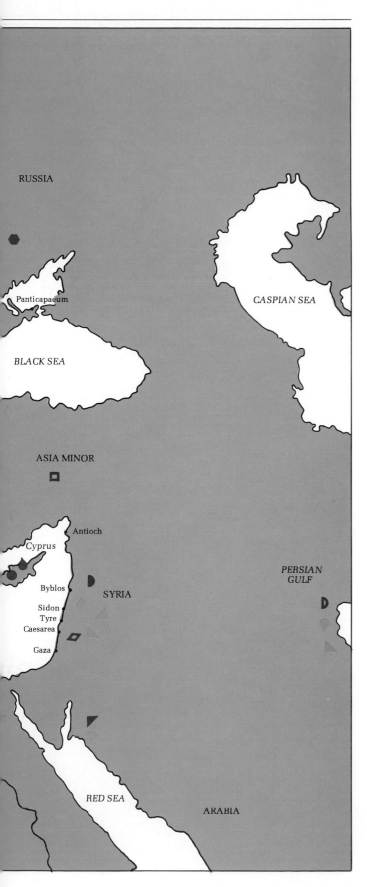

RUSSIA

Panticapaeum

CASPIAN SEA

BLACK SEA

ASIA MINOR

Antioch

Cyprus

PERSIAN
GULF

Byblos   SYRIA

Sidon
Tyre
Caesarea

Gaza

RED SEA

ARABIA

regular unit of 100 men; each such unit, called a *centuria*, was commanded by a *centurion*. The Roman sailor was so much a soldier that he called himself one—a *miles*; the Roman word for sailor, *nauta*, was not used by navy men.

But while the navy's organization was like that of the army, life aboard a Roman warship more nearly resembled that of a Greek warship. A *celeusta*, like the Greek *keleustes*, regulated the rate of stroke for the oarsmen. At the bow stood an officer who was in charge of the forward crew and watched out for shoals; another officer at the stern was responsible for the after part of the ship and the navigation. The commander of a large warship, called the *trierarchus*, had a staff of assistants, among them a clerk, a stenographer, a paymaster and a *scriba*, who wrote out regular reports to headquarters. To minister to the men's religious needs, some naval staffs also included a *coronarius* and a *victimarius*; their exact duties are unclear, but the *coronarius* may have been responsible for festooning the ship with wreaths for holidays, and the *victimarius* may have been charged with making sacrifices to the gods.

Rarely did the gods need to be thanked for victory in battle. During these years the only warfare consisted of pirate chasing, and pirates had been few and far between ever since Pompey had conducted his sweep of the Mediterranean in 67 B.C. Still, service aboard a Roman naval vessel was rigorous and promotion slow: Often a seaman would serve 10 years before stepping up in rank. The pay was modest, probably no better than that for provincial troops in the army. But the fleet normally put into harbor for the winter, and the crewmen might have earned extra money doing jobs ashore. Sailors skilled in handling heavy canvas, for instance, helped erect the awnings that shaded the spectators in amphitheaters; and when Roman citizens wanted a change from conventional gladiator fights, naval personnel might be called in to supervise the staging of mock sea battles.

These battles, called *naumachia*, were spectacular in both scale and vigor. During the reign of the First Century Emperor Claudius, for example, a huge sea fight was organized on the Fucine Lake, southeast of Rome. The surrounding slopes and hills were covered with spectators, while 19,000 criminals, armed like marines and sailing in galleys, fought one another in the center of the lake. Around them a circle of rafts, manned by double companies of the Praetorian Guard and fitted out with catapults and stone throwers, prevented the combatants from escaping. "Enough space in the middle," wrote the Roman historian Tacitus, "was left for energetic rowing, skillful steering, charging,

All sea roads led to Rome during her half millennium of dominance in the Mediterranean. Roman merchant ships brought amber from the Baltic and tin from Britain, lead from Spain and timber from North Africa, horses from Thrace and purple dye from Tyre, linen from Egypt and grain from Russia. Overland to the Mediterranean from the Red Sea came myrrh from the coast of East Africa and frankincense from Arabia. And by way of the Indian Ocean flowed ivory and spices from India and silk from the ports of China, some eight thousand miles away.

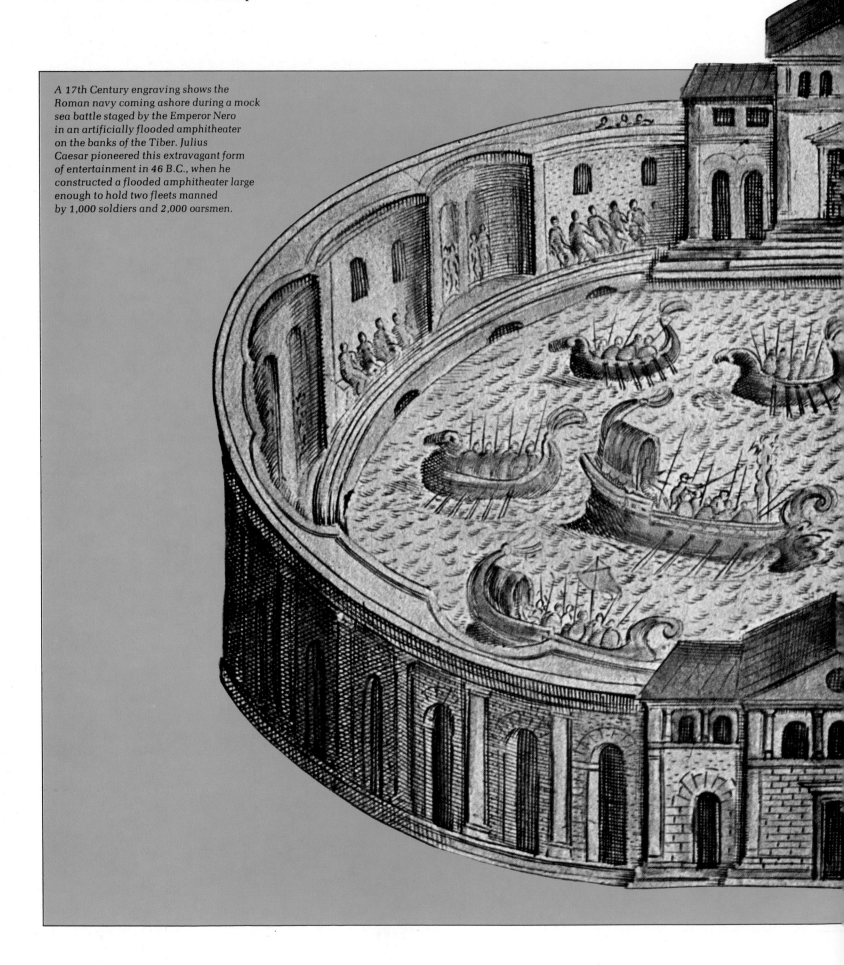

A 17th Century engraving shows the Roman navy coming ashore during a mock sea battle staged by the Emperor Nero in an artificially flooded amphitheater on the banks of the Tiber. Julius Caesar pioneered this extravagant form of entertainment in 46 B.C., when he constructed a flooded amphitheater large enough to hold two fleets manned by 1,000 soldiers and 2,000 oarsmen.

and all the incidents of a sea battle. Though the fighters were criminals, they fought like brave men. After much bloodletting, they were spared extermination."

If sea fighting was reduced to a charade during the great days of Empire, seagoing commerce attained a richness and complexity never before known. Like the imperial navy, the merchant marine was manned and organized by Greeks, Syrians and sailors from other ancient seafaring nations. Sometimes the ship's owner or charterer was his own captain; more often he handed the vessel over to an officer called the *magister navis,* who hired the crew and fitted out the ship, then delegated its navigation to a professional sailing master.

Merchant vessels were intrinsically the same as those used 500 years earlier—roomy and rotund, with a beam that was a quarter or even a third of their length. Fir, cedar and pine were favored for the planking, oak for the keel, and fir again for masts and yards. In most cases, the planks were joined carefully by mortises and tenons, and little calking was needed. Often the whole underwater surface was sheathed in lead.

It was in size, rather than in design, that the ships of this age differed from their predecessors. The great grain ships running between Rome and Alexandria stowed 1,200 tons of cargo and measured up to 180 feet in length. For more specialized transport, the Romans were capable of building true giants. In order to ship a 500-ton Egyptian obelisk from Alexandria to Rome, the Emperor Caligula ordered the construction of a vessel whose mainmast was reported to be more than 20 feet in circumference. Its ballast consisted of 800 tons of lentils; and while the exact length is not recorded, Pliny the Elder, author of Rome's standard encyclopedia, noted that the vessel "took up a large part of the left side of the harbor of Ostia," the port at the mouth of the Tiber. The huge transport had a unique second career: By order of the Emperor Claudius, it was sunk to form the base for a breakwater at the man-made harbor of Portus, just north of Ostia.

The average merchantman, with its matronly looking hull and a goose-head sternpost, moved over the sea with a certain portly dignity. Its hull was black, from being painted with pitch. (The few pirates still prowling the Mediterranean camouflaged their craft blue-gray.) A small cabin aft housed the captain, mates and any passengers of importance, while the rest—crew and passengers alike—passed the mild Mediterranean nights on deck or, in rainy weather, in the hold. In the hold, too, was stored the ship's drinking water and the crew's food; but most of the space was given over to cargo, to a ballast of stones or sand, and to the inevitable bilge water. On small craft the bilge was simply bailed out in buckets, but larger vessels had proper pumps.

The grander ships had two or even three decks and a stern galley where the cooking was done. The stern also held a latrine overhanging the sea, and the altar and image of the ship's guardian deity—Apollo, Aphrodite, or one of a variety of other gods. Often these deities lent their names to the ships, and this name was carved or painted on either side of the bow. On the stern of one huge freighter was a splendidly decorated chapel, dedicated to Aphrodite.

An illustrious victim of Vesuvius

When Mount Vesuvius started its most famous eruption on August 24, 79 A.D., the commander of the Roman naval base at nearby Cape Misenum was Pliny the Elder, author of a monumental encyclopedia and a man who regarded the world with almost legendary curiosity. Though obese and asthmatic at the age of 56, Pliny promptly set sail for the volcano in a fleet of warships. Dictating precise scientific notes on the phenomenon, Pliny landed at Stabiae, four miles south of Pompeii. There he dined in a friend's villa, and endeavored to calm his host's fears by stoically sleeping while the sky rained ash and pumice and Vesuvius' blasts shook the villa and stirred the sea.

By morning they were almost entombed. The commander's nephew, Pliny the Younger, recounts that, in daylight that was "blacker and denser than any night that ever was," his uncle went down to the shore to "investigate on the spot the possibility of any escape by sea, but he found the waves still wild and dangerous." While his companions fled from the fiery bombardment, the elder Pliny remained, leaning on two slaves until he collapsed, choked by the thick, sulphurous fumes. Two days later, his nephew relates, "his body was found intact and uninjured, still fully clothed and looking more like sleep than death." The fate of the two slaves is unrecorded, but in Pompeii itself, 2,000 residents died in Vesuvius' engulfing eruption.

Merchant ships were dominated by a broad square sail, sewed together from pieces of canvas, bordered by bolt ropes, and held to the mast by a long yard. A rectangular topsail and, on larger ships, a small mizzen helped drive the vessel. Steering was facilitated by a spritsail that was sharply raked over the bows. The ropes of the elaborate rigging—halyards, braces, brails, lifts—were made of hemp, flax, twisted papyrus or even strips of leather.

The rig was best suited to a following wind, and any speed of more than four knots was considered excellent. In one record voyage, a ship sailed from Ostia to a point off Cap Bon in Tunisia in two days—an average speed of almost six knots for the 270 miles. Another fast-traveling merchantman, running before the northwest winds, covered the 830 miles between Sicily and Egypt in only six days—again an average of nearly six knots. On the other hand, if a vessel had to tack into the prevailing winds, progress was miserably slow. The 250 miles between Alexandria and Cyprus might take almost a week; and the Roman writer Sulpicius Severus reported that he was happy to have reached

In a 19th Century French painting, Pliny the Elder, supported by his slaves, slumps to the beach as Vesuvius' ash sifts down.

Marseilles from Egypt in 30 days—an average speed of two knots.

Other merchant craft—used mainly for perishable cargoes or for cruising in coastal regions where winds from all directions would be encountered—were powered by oars as well as by sail. Bulkier than war galleys, sleeker than sailing ships, these merchant galleys came into their own when becalmed or when entering port. On occasions when contrary winds might force a sailing ship to linger outside a dangerous harbor mouth for days, the merchant galley could run out her oars and pull in to a safe anchorage.

By the Second Century A.D. the whole Mediterranean was ringed by well-protected harbors. Some ports—Syracuse, Tyre and Alexandria among them—had twin basins, each oriented a different way so that ships might enter easily no matter what the wind direction. Enormous moles shouldered their way into the sea and shielded the anchorage; one at Alexandria measured more than half a mile in length. To construct these masonry breakwaters, the Romans used a concrete that would set underwater.

Within the port's encircling arms, merchantmen tied up bows on at stone quays lined with porticoes and backed by warehouses. Along the quays, the scene resembled that of Athens' Piraeus five centuries earlier, though on a grander scale. The wharves were inundated by clerks, port officials and a seething river of stevedores—men who toted sacks of grain and amphorae of wine or oil that weighed as much as 100 pounds. A single ship might bring in 3,000 amphorae, or chunks of building stone weighing 20 tons that had to be winched onto carts or barges by sturdy revolving cranes.

The biggest man-made harbor in the ancient world was Portus, begun by the Emperor Claudius in 42 A.D. on the marshy coast two miles north of the Tiber's mouth. Two gigantic breakwaters, each more than 2,500 feet long and 50 feet wide, curled out into the sea to enclose an anchorage of 160 acres. The southernmost mole, massed against prevailing winds and a current that swept the Tiber's silt northward, was underpinned in part by the colossal obelisk-carrying ship sunk there by Claudius.

Near the harbor entrance, some 400 feet wide, a mammoth lighthouse rose in three square stories of diminishing size, topped by a cylindrical tower that held a statue of Neptune and a blazing beacon. Into this harbor sailed ships bearing goods from all over the known world. Their cargoes were transferred to barges that were pulled along a canal to the Tiber and thence 15 miles upriver to the docks of Rome. In some years the port's handle of grain alone amounted to about half a million tons.

For all its massive breakwaters, the harbor was open to an occasional northwesterly storm. In 62 A.D., 200 ships were wrecked as they rode at anchor there. So between 101 and 104 A.D., the Emperor Trajan scooped out an inner haven, connected to the old anchorage by a short channel. Trajan's creation was a landlocked, hexagonal harbor of 78 acres. Surrounded by temples, warehouses, baths, an imperial palace and even a tiny theater, it had mooring facilities for more than 100 ships.

As Portus boomed, so did the older, neighboring port of Ostia. It housed not only many of the workers of Portus, but also most of its

Harvest of the wild

Among the most exotic of the Roman merchant fleet's imports were wild animals that were fated to be participants in cruel and spectacular entertainments. Elephants, rhinoceroses, crocodiles, hippopotamuses, lions and tigers were brought to Rome by the thousands, there to amuse the populace in two ways: staged hunts in which the animals were killed with spears or bows and arrows; and grisly exhibitions in which animals were loosed in the arena to fight to the death, either with humans or with one another.

As far as Roman audiences were concerned, the more carnage the better. In 26 spectacles staged by Augustus Caesar, 3,500 animals were massacred. When the Emperor Titus inaugurated the Colosseum in 80 A.D., 9,000 were slaughtered. And Trajan out-did them all: A grand total of 11,000 beasts died in celebration of his triumph over Dacia (modern Rumania) in 105 A.D. This wholesale sacrifice of animals lasted for seven centuries, and it helped alter forever the fauna of many regions of the Empire. Elephants had disappeared from North Africa by the Fourth Century A.D.

The animals' capture is vividly illustrated in a Third Century A.D. mosaic entitled "The Big Game Hunt," shown in part here and on the following pages. An example of the so-called continuous style of Roman narrative art, it depicts animals simultaneously being hunted, loaded on vessels and unloaded for the trek to the arenas where they were to die so dramatically.

A detail from "The Big Game Hunt" mosaic is an example of the simultaneous action by which the artist tried to tell a continuous story of importing animals to Rome. While an African elephant is prodded up the gangway of a ship, the foot and tail of another animal are visible as it leaves the vessel at its destination.

In a segment from the mosaic, a merchant vessel is being loaded with a gazelle-like animal and a pair of ostriches, as four hunters—two of them toting a boar slung in a net, the others carrying a crated animal—stride toward the ship. At bottom left an officer apparently threatens to punish a laggard helper.

Another phase of the animal roundup pictured by the artist focuses on two hunters, one mounted (left) and another with a shield (top right) directing his men toward the quarry—a leopard (top left) and a lioness feeding on antelopes. At bottom, oxen pull a cart loaded with crates to transport the animals.

business and administrative agencies. Hefty brick apartment buildings, some of them five stories high, shared the streets with temples, granaries, wine shops and bars. Ostia became wealthy in a modest, middle-class way. It resembled a smaller version of Rome, with a privileged upper class of wealthy merchants and bankers, a large middle class that managed the port and its services, and a lowest class of slaves who provided the labor. But Ostia was no suburb of Rome; indeed, it had its own suburb, with the residential villas of the wealthy dotting the coastline south of the city.

The guilds of Ostia and Portus reveal some of the activities of the dockside world. These guilds were primarily fraternal organizations based on shared business interests, rather than trade unions in the modern sense. Members were elected, and they included employers as well as workers. There were guilds not only for different trades—in grain, wine and oil above all—and for such prestigious professions as shipbuilders (whose roll of 353 members in the late Second Century included the name of a woman), but also for most workers in the ports: warehousemen, stevedores, salvage divers, "sandmen" who provided ships' ballast, grain measurers and the owners of various sorts of small workaday craft.

Such guilds, and all the commercial apparatus of the seafaring world, flourished mightily during the two centuries of peace that followed the accession of Augustus Caesar. Under the protection of Roman arms, the whole Empire saw a flood of merchants coming and going with a variety of goods unequaled before. Even beyond the reach of the Roman sword, Rome's agents were respected. They sailed to Ireland and the Baltic Sea, traded along the shores of Ethiopia and voyaged eastward into the Indian Ocean as far as Malaya. Over the length and breadth of the Mediterranean the beamy merchantmen, driven by their huge, simple spread of sail, might carry Spanish fish sauce, Cornish tin, marinated Cypriote songbirds, Athenian statuary (for the courtyards of the *nouveaux riches*), Russian furs, and Numidian slaves.

The Roman entrepreneurs who orchestrated these intricate cycles of exchange were immortalized—less than lovingly—by Petronius, the acid-tongued arbiter of etiquette during Nero's reign. One of his most memorable creations is the fictional figure of Trimalchio, an ex-slave who had become a multimillionaire through trade. Bragging to his dinner guests, Trimalchio uses a parvenu's phraseology that can be loosely translated as: "I built myself five ships, loaded them with wine—which was worth its weight in gold at the time—and sent them to Rome. Every single one of them was wrecked, that's the god's honest truth; Neptune gulped down a cool 30 million in one day. I built myself some more, got hold of another cargo of wine, added bacon, beans, a load of slaves . . . the little woman sold all her jewels to raise the cash. I netted a cool ten million on that one voyage."

Trimalchio survived the financial disaster of shipwreck with no great trouble, but many a merchant was ruined that way. Moreover, if a merchant could not pay off his creditors, he might be thrown in jail—and have to stay there until he had found a way to raise more money. One imprisoned merchant found himself sharing a cell with a convict who was about to be executed for murder. Taking pity on his cellmate, the murderer revealed where he had hidden some of his ill-gotten treasure. The merchant told his wife, who went to the spot and unearthed enough to set her husband free to trade again.

To Rome's merchants, however, the rewards were well worth the risks, for the trading opportunities were endless. From Britain came cattle, slaves, geese (a great delicacy) and fierce hunting dogs. Germany offered precious amber, while the provinces of Gaul produced cereals for export, as well as woolen garments, hides, vegetables, fish, poultry and flax. These were floated down Gaul's great rivers—principally the Rhone—to the Mediterranean, together with pottery and glass, wine, hams and pickled pork, and found their way all over the Roman world. As far away as Palestine, King Herod Agrippa talked of the Gauls as "flooding the whole world with their goods."

Spain had a prodigious endowment of minerals—iron, gold, silver and lead mines—all owned by the state. Contractors leased the mines and used slaves to work them. In addition, Spain exported agricultural products: olive oil, wool (its black sheep were famous), flax for cloth weaving and for sails and nets, and grass for cordage.

To the east, Greece exported beautiful building materials: the veined and greenish marbles of the southern Peloponnesus, the glowing white marble of Athens, the variegated marbles of the islands. Greek honey from Mount Hymettus, made by bees feeding on thyme, was famous too, as was Greek olive oil, fit even for the Emperor's table. Horses were shipped from the plains of Thessaly in the north, while copper and smelted bronze came from Cyprus. Greece also provided the inspiration for much of Rome's burgeoning culture. The Greek language was favored by scholars, and Homer was considered by Roman readers to be the greatest of all poets, though Rome's own Vergil won some prominence in the Latin-speaking areas of the Empire. The books themselves were usually made with papyrus from Egypt, and were written on a continuous roll, as they had been in earlier cultures. Not until the Fourth Century did the roll give way to the codex—sheets bound in book form.

East of Greece, the long, rocky coastline of Asia Minor seethed with trade. Its products were often obscure but valuable: truffles, resinous gums, goat-hair cloaks and leggings, beeswax. For medicinal purposes, the sulphides, saffron, wild spikenard and mastic of Asia Minor were coveted everywhere; its prunes and damsons reached the richest tables of Rome; its wool, from the great city of Miletus, was second to none; and on the Black Sea coast the Pontic forests were felled and transported to be used for ships' timbers.

North Africa supplied ebony and citrus woods (used to make furniture), as well as grain and olives; much of the grain was now exported from Carthage, which had been rebuilt by Julius Caesar and had grown wealthy again. From farther south came ivory, ostrich feathers, rhinoceros horn—and slaves. The flow of slaves into Rome during the First and Second Centuries A.D. was a trickle compared to what war had yielded in earlier times. But imperial Rome did not lack for them. Pliny the Younger—son of the encyclopedist and a noted author in his own right—had at least 500; in his will he freed 100 of them, the maximum allowed by law. Slaves were so numerous, in fact, that when some senators proposed that they be required to wear special clothing, the proposal was rejected because it was feared that the slaves would become aware of their own strength.

Slaves played an important part in the development of the Empire. Augustus created an imperial bureaucracy manned almost entirely by slaves, since such work was considered demeaning by free Romans, and his approach to civil service staffing was followed throughout the Empire using both slaves and freedmen (slaves who were eventually given their freedom—and many were). Freedmen were permitted to go into business, and thousands of them amassed fortunes and bought their own

The anchors of antiquity

An indispensable part of the ancient mariner's gear was an anchor to secure his ship against wind and current while it was in harbor or off a lee shore during a storm. Initially, anchors were simply heavy stones with a hole for attaching the cables; some of these elementary anchors had additional holes to support wooden stakes that helped the device hold fast.

By Roman times, anchors had become more sophisticated. One type *(far right)* had a wooden shank and a lead stock—a crosspiece that allowed the anchor to fall at an angle so the arms would dig in. Another type *(center)* was made entirely of iron, sometimes with the shank and arms sheathed in wood—possibly for esthetic reasons. The stock of such anchors might be removable to permit flat stowage on deck.

FOURTH CENTURY B.C. STONE ANCHORS

WOOD-SHEATHED IRON ANCHOR WITH REMOVABLE STOCK

WOODEN ANCHOR WITH LEAD STOCK

slaves. Moreover, the Emperor Claudius extended the full rights of citizenship to freedmen who invested their capital in outfitting merchant ships. Nero provided the same inducement to those who put their money into shipbuilding.

Rome attracted other live imports. Peacocks, brought from India, graced Roman banquet tables. And whole boatloads of leopards, lions and panthers captured in Africa and Asia Minor were shipped to Rome (pages 141-144) for bloody spectacles in the amphitheaters. Many perished on the long voyages; those that survived were penned in enormous menageries to await slaughter in the arena. Only a few were tamed and taught tricks for less sanguinary entertainment.

A favorite diversion in the amphitheater was an unequal contest between these animals, usually starved for the occasion, and humans, often barehanded. Condemnation to this death was at first reserved for foreigners who had deserted from the army or navy. But the sentence was eventually extended to other lowborn miscreants, including runaway or mutinous slaves, and to Christians who refused to acknowledge Rome's state religion and offer sacrifices in homage to the Emperor. With absurd decorum, the statues adorning the amphitheaters were veiled, to be spared the grisly spectacle.

In the First Century the Emperor Claudius worked at expanding Roman shipping and made many visits to Ostia, the port at the mouth of the Tiber. When Ostia's limited facilities exacerbated a grain shortage in Rome, he ordered the digging of a modern harbor nearby—to be called Portus.

After the walls of the new harbor of Portus were breached by storms in 104 A.D., the Emperor Trajan commissioned the design of an annex—an inner, more carefully protected harbor connected to the outer anchorage. Trajan also widened the canal linking Portus to the Tiber.

The satirist Juvenal maintained that the Romans were interested only in bread and circuses. Whether true or not, their astute rulers saw that they got plenty of both. Before the time of Christ, politicians seeking favor with the people had started to subsidize grain supplies, and what was once simply a vote-winning tactic soon became a necessity. For three centuries after Christ, the 200,000 poor who lived in Rome (the city's total population was about a million) were accustomed to receive a dole either of free grain or of grain sold below the market price and, later, even of wine and pork.

Sicily, North Africa and Egypt all shouldered the burden of feeding the mother city; their grain was extracted from them as a tax. But the long, fertile Nile Valley became the grain supplier of the Empire. Augustus had been quick to see Egypt's potential, and he moved to exploit it for his own advantage. After his defeat of Antony and Cleopatra, he posed as the divine successor to the Ptolemies and appointed a carefully selected prefect as his agent in charge of the government. He then concentrated on turning the area into a vast granary, collecting the grain as tribute from the Egyptian farmers and storing it in Alexandrian warehouses for shipment to Rome. Augustus even forbade Roman senators and others of high rank to enter Alexandria without his permission, piously claiming that the religious orgies of the East would corrupt their morals; his real purpose was to keep this lucrative monopoly under tight control and to strengthen his hold over the grain-hungry masses at home.

The Alexandrian grain fleet that carried the produce received solicitous attention from the Emperors. Augustus passed laws that penalized anyone hindering the grain ships. The Emperor Claudius, on one occasion finding only 15 days' grain supply in the silos of Rome, promised bounties to any grain ship sailing in the stormy winter months (most other merchantmen stayed off the sea lanes from mid-November to mid-March). By the time of Trajan, who ruled from 98 to 117 A.D., 150,000

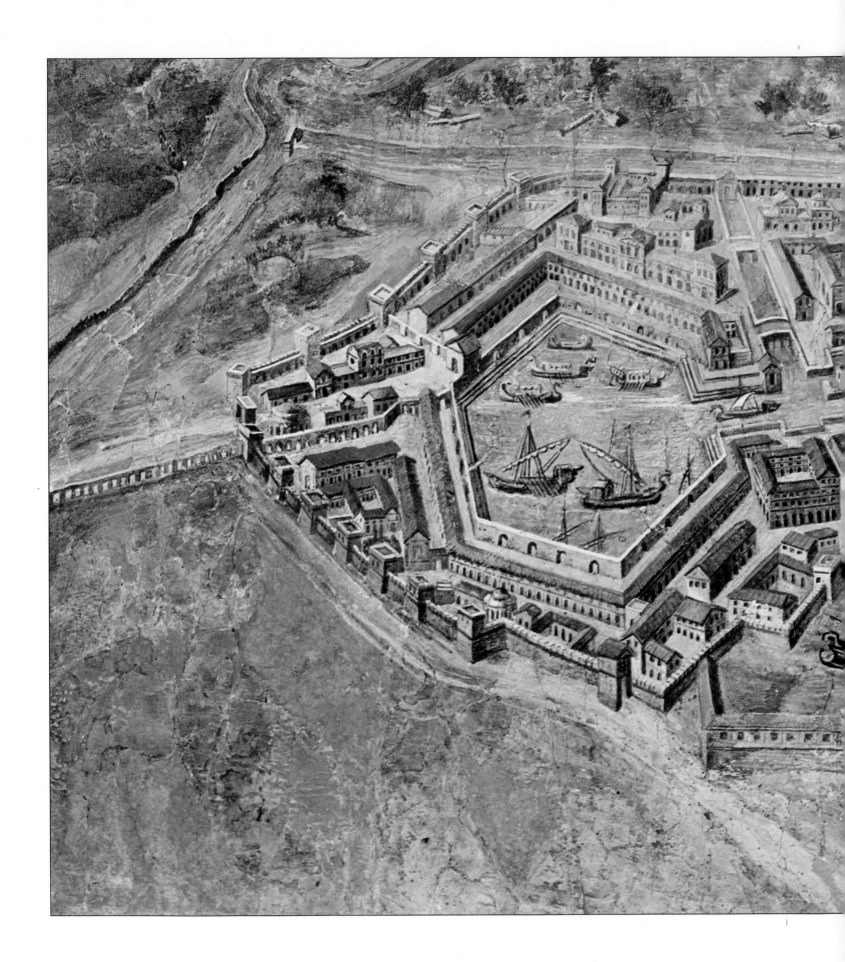

The man-made complex of Portus is reproduced—with little attention to scale—in this 16th Century painting. The outer basin, guarded at its entrance by a lighthouse and a huge statue of Neptune, could accommodate merchant vessels with a 12- to 15-foot draft (Ostia, silted up by the Tiber's mud, could handle only shallow-draft vessels). Fully 300 ships could dock at the wharves of this outer basin. The hexagonal inner basin had a 78-acre anchorage surrounded by wharves and warehouses.

tons of grain were being carried yearly from Egypt to Rome. The fleet, numbering perhaps 85 giant vessels, sailed on a regular schedule.

From Italy to Egypt the trip was fast. Ships would depart in April and ride the trade winds all the way to their destination, usually taking two or three weeks. Their captains, declared the Emperor Caligula, "drive them like racehorses." Then, heavy with grain, they would labor back against the prevailing winds from the northwest, island-hopping to Cyprus, through the Aegean and across to Malta, or moving due west along the Libyan coast before crossing to Sicily. The voyage home might take two months. "Today the ships from Alexandria suddenly came into view," wrote the Roman man of letters Lucius Seneca from the port of Pozzuoli, near Naples, in the First Century. "It is a welcome sight to the country. The whole mob at Pozzuoli stands on the docks; they can recognize the ships from Alexandria, even in a crowd of vessels, by their sails. For, though all ships carry topsails on the open water, these are the only ones allowed to keep them up."

Not every voyage went smoothly, of course. One tempest-battered grain ship traveling between Rome and Alexandria was blown north and, after 70 days at sea, put in at Piraeus. Many of Piraeus' inhabitants had never seen such a vessel before, and an onlooker recorded his amazement in some detail:

"What a size the ship was! One hundred and eighty feet in length, the ship's carpenter told me, the beam more than a quarter of that, and 44 feet from the deck to the lowest point in the hold. And the height of the mast, and what a yard it carried, and what a forestay they had to use to hold it up! And the way the stern rose up in a gradual curve ending in a gilded goose head, matched at the other end by the forward, more flattened, sweep of the prow with its figures of Isis, the goddess the ship was named after, on each side! Everything was incredible: the rest of the decoration, the paintings, the red topsail, even more, the anchors with their capstans and winches, and the cabins aft. The crew was like an army. They told me she carried enough grain to feed every mouth in Athens for a year. And it all depends for its safety on one little old man who turns those great steering oars with a tiller that's no more than a stick! They pointed him out to me; woolly-haired little fellow, half bald; Heron was his name, I think."

These great ships were passenger carriers, too: Some could accommodate as many as 600 travelers. Most of the passengers were businessmen—shippers, traders or their agents traveling from one port to another. But as they grew prosperous, the Romans became inveterate tourists. Egypt, spectacularly endowed with its pyramids and temples, was the most popular destination, and Greece a close second. Roman scholars, who regarded Greece as the fountain of civilization, flocked on grand tours through the Hellenic antiquities at Athens, Olympia and Delphi. The Aegean islands of Chios, Lesbos and Samos were oft-visited, too, and the Colossus at the harbor entrance of Rhodes still attracted tourists, even though it had been leveled by an earthquake in the Third Century B.C. and lay on the ground in ruins.

Egypt's great attraction was its gleaming city of Alexandria, and the tourists also enjoyed floating along the Nile to visit cities more ancient

Rome relied on the rest of the Empire for the bulk of its food supply, and each precious shipment of grain was painstakingly measured on arrival, as evidenced by this mosaic. At left, a young clerk signals a slave to bring a sack of grain, which will be dumped into a regulation container. At center, an official inspects the contents of the measure and holds aloft a stick used to level off the grain. Slaves at right wait to empty the container so that the process can continue.

than their own, while admiring the spectacular pyramids along the way. One of the wonders of the world to Roman tourists apparently was the ruins of Egypt's huge statue of Amenophis III, which occasionally emitted a melodious sound like the plucking of a lyre string. Extensive Latin graffiti inscribed on the remnants are evidence of the statue's popularity.

In accordance with the social custom of the day, the distinguished residents of the provinces extended hospitality to touring Roman officials. This custom put a financial strain on the most frequently visited locales of the Empire. Romans, for example, flocked to the African seaside town of Hippo Zarytus, which boasted a unique special attraction—a tame dolphin that sported in the water with children. When acting as hosts for the hordes of visitors became a ruinous financial burden, the desperate town fathers killed the dolphin.

Many Romans went abroad for their health. Some traveled to Epidaurus on the Greek island of Kos, where Hippocrates had founded a school of medicine centuries before. In the Second Century A.D. a pow-

erful lure was Pergamon, south of Constantinople, where the great physician Galen held court. Visitors to Pergamon began their therapy by taking a purifying bath, praying in the temple of Asclepius—the god of healing—and lying on a pallet to sleep; their dreams, interpreted by the local priests, were supposed to indicate a cure—which usually turned out to be certain foods and unguents, exercises or more ritual baths. Some Romans preferred spas like Aquae Calidae (present-day Vichy) in France or Aquae Aureliae (Baden Baden) in Germany for their supposedly health-restoring waters.

Despite the amount of travel done by Romans, Portus and Ostia offered no regular passenger lines or agents. The prospective tourist simply booked passage on the first available merchant ship headed for his destination. Since most of the ship's hold would be reserved for its cargo, the traveler often had to settle for space on deck. He purchased a collapsible shelter to shield him from the elements, and brought with him a slave or

A Third Century relief depicts Roman stevedores unloading amphorae, the two-handled jars used to transport olive oil and wine by sea. On the quay (right) one shipping clerk hands a stevedore a tally, while the others record the delivery. The average merchant vessel could carry some 3,000 amphorae, each with a capacity of about six gallons.

two to look after his comfort. Spending a few weeks on deck was generally far preferable to traveling over Roman roads, whether on foot, donkeyback, in a wooden-wheeled carriage or even—for the extravagant—in a litter borne by slaves.

Sea travel had its dangers, of course. In 61 A.D. a ship carrying 600 passengers sank in the Adriatic. Only 80 survived, by swimming all night until a passing vessel rescued them in the morning. The poet Terence is thought to have perished on his way back from Greece in 159 B.C.; some say he drowned, others that he died of grief because he lost his baggage, which contained new translations of 108 plays by the Greek playwright Menander.

The worst risk at sea came from sailing at the wrong season, as Saint Paul learned in 62 A.D. Arrested for sedition, he was put aboard a grain ship bound for Rome to be tried before Caesar. It was already late in the sailing season, however, and when the vessel reached Crete, the owner and the captain decided to winter there. The ship did not put into port soon enough: "There arose against it a tempestuous wind, called Euroclydon [a northeast gale]," runs the Acts of the Apostles. "And when the ship was caught, and could not bear up into the wind, we let her drive." In this situation, even the huge grain carrier was helpless. The sailors slung hawsers under her hull to keep her from breaking up, then struck sail and committed themselves to the mercy of the wind. For 14 days they were driven helplessly before the storm. On the first day they threw overboard everything superfluous; on the third day they dismantled part of the rigging. "And when neither sun nor stars in many days appeared, and no small tempest lay on us, all hope that we should be saved was then taken away."

On the 14th night the sailors dropped plummets to gauge the sea's depth; they found it to be only 20 fathoms. They were nearing land, but were able to see only the lowering blackness of the sky and the thrashing waves. They sounded again. Now the depth was only 15 fathoms. The sea was shoaling fast; at any moment they might hit rocks. So, praying for daylight, they cast out their four stern anchors. The sailors lowered their ship's boat into the dark waters, planning to make their way to shore and abandon the 276 passengers aboard. However, at the last moment they decided not to continue with this perfidious—and perilous—scheme. They cut the boat loose, jettisoned the grain to lighten ship and waited for the dawn.

"And when it was day," the Acts of the Apostles continues, "they knew not the land: but they discovered a certain creek with a shore, into the which they were minded, if it were possible, to thrust in the ship. And when they had taken up the anchors, they committed themselves unto the sea, and loosed the rudder bands." With the mainsail hoisted to the winds, the ship was caught by two converging currents and driven ashore. Her bow struck firm, holding fast. Astern, the seams cracked and the waves rushed in.

Saint Paul and everyone else aboard were saved. Their landfall was Malta. Three months later another grain ship, whose captain had wisely put in earlier for the winter, carried Saint Paul on to Rome—and to his eventual execution.

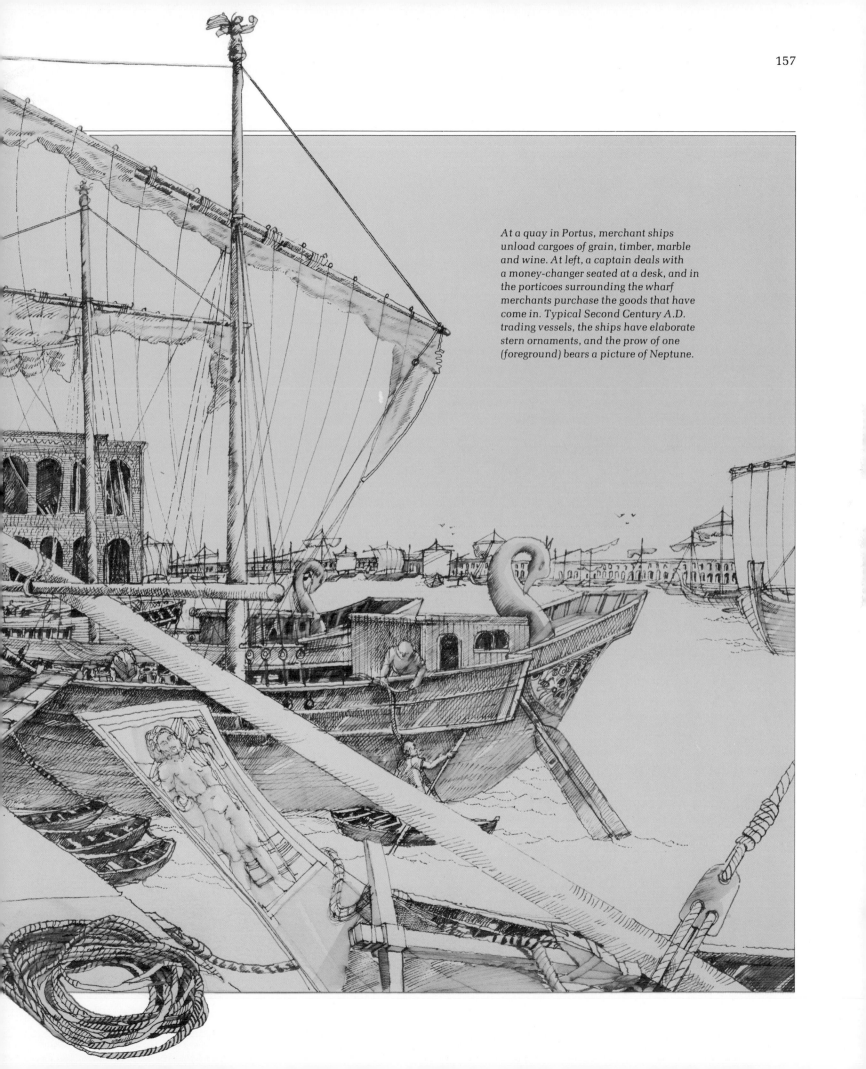

At a quay in Portus, merchant ships unload cargoes of grain, timber, marble and wine. At left, a captain deals with a money-changer seated at a desk, and in the porticoes surrounding the wharf merchants purchase the goods that have come in. Typical Second Century A.D. trading vessels, the ships have elaborate stern ornaments, and the prow of one (foreground) bears a picture of Neptune.

The Mediterranean was the heart of the Roman world, but the Empire's maritime net was flung more widely. Additional riches for Rome were brought by ships plying the routes to Arabia, Persia and India.

"The sun shone over the open terraces, over the warehouses near the harbor and over the turrets with windows like the eyes of deer. In different places of Puhar, the onlooker's attention was caught by the sight of the abodes of Yavanas, whose prosperity never waned. At the harbor were to be seen sailors from many lands, but to all appearances they lived as one community."

Thus an Indian poet in Roman times described the port of Puhar, where the Cauvery River flows into the Bay of Bengal. "Yavanas" was a word for Westerners trading for Rome—Greeks or Egyptians whose "beautifully built ships," wrote another poet, "came with gold and returned with pepper."

As early as the reign of Augustus, more than 100 merchant ships a year sailed to East African and Indian ports. And envoys from India had arrived in the Mediterranean. A royal Punjabi delegation brought Augustus an exotic selection of marvels: a man born without arms, a river turtle, an outsized partridge, a collection of snakes, and a fanatical holy man who proceeded to immolate himself in flames. Early in the First Century, the King of Ceylon sent envoys to the Emperor Claudius; Roman trade soon extended to the island. And as late as the Fourth Century, Constantine the Great was receiving ambassadors from India.

So trade with the East—a modest flow of goods in Hellenistic times—became a flood. Augustus' successor, the Emperor Tiberius, even introduced sumptuary laws to restrict the exchange of Western bullion for Eastern luxuries. "The ladies and their baubles are transferring our money to foreigners," he grumbled.

One of the most coveted commodities of the East was Arabian incense, which rose in sweet-smelling and expensive clouds from the altars of all the Roman world. Not only was it offered up daily by devout Romans to their household gods, but it was also used in public processions of state and religious festivals, especially during animal sacrifices: The incense was sprinkled over the head of the victim, mingled with its blood and poured into the flames.

The finest incense was made from the resin of shrubs and trees that grew on Arabia's southern coast. The Arabs had so much of it that they thought nothing of burning the most expensive and fragrant woods—cinnamon and cassia, as well as frankincense and myrrh—in their household fires. "When they are made drowsy by the sweet odors," wrote the geographer Strabo, "they overcome the drowsiness by inhaling the incense of asphalt and goatsbeard."

A second great commodity of the East was Chinese silk. In the Third Century A.D. it was literally worth its weight in gold. Its manufacture was a secret jealously guarded by the Chinese—and would remain so until the Sixth Century, when Byzantine monks returned to the West with silkworm eggs concealed in a staff head. At first the excessive use of silk was discouraged by Rome's Emperors; but wealthy Romans found the soft, shimmering material irresistible, and silk-decorated curtains, cushions and clothing became status symbols of the upper classes.

Advertisements underfoot

An ingenious form of advertising—billboards on the floor—played an important role in Rome's port of Ostia during the Third Century A.D. When a trader wanted to purchase imports, ship out his own goods or go on a voyage, he visited the Forum of the Corporations, a huge, colonnaded square that was the focal point of commerce in Ostia. At its center stood a temple dedicated to Ceres, goddess of agriculture and food supply, and around its sides were scores of offices maintained by *navicularii*—shipowners who carried goods between the ports of the Empire. If the trader was unsure where to find the particular shipowner he sought, he simply walked around the perimeter of the square, studying the pavement. Mosaics embedded in the sidewalk proclaimed the port or country at the other end of a shipper's route *(right)*.

The *navicularii* were rigidly regulated by officers representing Rome's Prefect of Annona, the functionary responsible for all the city's food supplies; these officers inspected the shipper's goods on arrival and supervised their storage and distribution. But the government was as generous as it was strict. It supplied the *navicularii's* ships, sometimes paid for repairs, and insured any cargoes belonging to the state. As for fees, the *navicularii* received a percentage of the value of the cargoes they carried—which included a staggering total of 15 million bushels of grain each year.

Masonry columns (below) divided the Forum of the Corporations into 78 rooms. A shipper's office might have as many as three rooms, with one mosaic out front.

NAVI NARBONINSES

A ship sailing up to a lighthouse at a harbor entrance is featured on the mosaic advertisement of one Ostia shipper (above); words atop the scene indicate that this shipowner's base is Narbonne, the capital of southern Gaul. In the mosaic advertisement at right, two stylized vessels are identified as belonging to shipowners of Carthage. Rebuilt after its destruction in the Punic Wars, Carthage had become a major source of grain shipments by the Third Century A.D.

NAVICVL KARTHAG DE SVO

A third prized Eastern product was pepper. In the Roman Empire this became the paramount spice for seasoning food—at first a luxury, then a necessity. It grew in three kinds: the long pepper, which consisted of pod-enclosed seeds; the black, which was harvested as unripe berries; and the white, the ripened version of the black. All three types were cultivated in southern and central India and were at first a rarity in the West; as late as 13 B.C. the poet Horace wrote of pepper as being very scarce. But by the end of the First Century, it was being used in almost every Roman recipe, and the Emperor Vespasian built special warehouses for storing supplies in Rome. Along with pepper came ginger, spikenard, cinnamon and many other Eastern spices, which were used not only in food but in medicine (as was pepper itself) and in perfumes, cosmetics and incense.

Two great trade routes brought silk and spices to Rome. The first was a complex inland trail that traversed the steppes of Central Asia north of the Himalayas and crossed the Persian desert to the Mediterranean coast of Syria. But the belligerent Parthian dynasty that ruled Persia between 223 B.C. and 226 A.D. was hostile to Rome and frequently threatened this route. Consequently, a second avenue became popular: The precious Eastern commodities traveled across the Indian Ocean, up the Red Sea, overland from the Red Sea ports to the Nile, and down the Nile to the Mediterranean. This route posed dangers, too: Corsairs based along the shores of Arabia were a menace. Toward the end of the First Century B.C. the Romans tried to conquer the petty Arabian kingdoms in order to quell piracy, but their expeditions were unsuccessful. At any given time, therefore, merchants opted for whichever was the lesser of two evils: When the pirates became too troublesome, they used the land route; and when the hostile Parthians stepped up their attacks, the traders would turn back to the sea route.

The key to the sea route was the alternating character of the monsoon winds in the Indian Ocean and the Arabian Sea. From May to September the winds blow from the southwest, and a ship captain could ride them across to India. For the rest of the year the winds conveniently blow in the opposite direction, allowing ships to speed back to the Red Sea. Until late in the Second Century B.C., Greek and Egyptian mariners trading with the East were unaware of the monsoon phenomenon. Instead, they hugged the Arabian coast from the Red Sea to the Persian Gulf, paying tolls in Arabian ports along the way; at the mouth of the Indus River, they turned southeast and sailed on to India's rich Malabar coast and even as far as the island of Ceylon. A Greek captain named Hippalus finally learned of the monsoon's behavior (it had long been known to Arabian and Indian seamen, who kept it a secret), and soon Western traders were regularly sailing straight across the Arabian Sea, avoiding both Arabian toll collectors and pirates. The voyage to the Malabar coast and back to Egypt—7,000 miles in all—could be made within a year.

Despite its remoteness from the Mediterranean, this is the best-known of the ancient trade routes, because at some point in the First Century A.D. an unknown Greek sea captain described it in exhaustive detail, offering information on harbors, tides, winds, local inhabitants and the products of the ports along the way. He called his book *The Periplus of*

Flood tide of seaborne luxury

Rome's Augustan age was a period of unprecedented opulence, fostered by a trading network that drew on the resources of almost the entire known world. Wealthy Romans adorned their mansions and villas with veined marble shipped from Greece and filled them with furniture made of fine woods imported from Asia Minor and inlaid with gold or silver from Spain. In such elegant surroundings a Roman banquet would be served on plates fashioned from gold, with wine poured from chased-silver ewers. The evening's delicacies might be pheasants' or peacocks' brains and flamingos' tongues, brought from Spain or the Aegean.

The diners, men as well as women, covered their clothes, fingers and even hair with rubies, sapphires and pearls brought from the Orient. So avid were Romans for jewelry that some hosts were said to station a slave behind each guest to make sure he or she did not pry the gems from the cup in the course of the dinner.

Silver, presumably from the mines of Spain, was used to make this commodious two-handled wine vessel, delicately decorated with hunting scenes (right) and a man straining at the oars of a skiff.

At the bottom of an Alexandrian cup made of onyx, a cameo relief includes a personification of the Nile River (left) and Hellenized versions of Egyptian divinities. The scene celebrates the annual flood of the Nile basin.

Designed to keep foods warm over a flame, this tray is made of bronze, presumably from Italy's bronze works. Both the tray and its implements have handles and legs of Greek design.

Delicately carved legs with a winged Egyptian motif hold a ceremonial tripod table (right) of wrought bronze. It was found in the ruins of a temple at Pompeii.

Made of bronze inlaid with silver and gold, this elegant stool is embellished with a carved head (center) of the Greek mythological monster Medusa.

Olive oil, a major import from Greece and North Africa, was burned in the two slipper-shaped lamps of this Roman candelabrum, whose base is a bronze figure of Silenus, a follower of the Greek god of wine, Bacchus.

A tall, elaborately decorated wine vessel stands on its own tripod. The blue glass of the wine vessel is overlaid with opaque white figures of cupids harvesting grapes for the wine press.

A Roman noblewoman could compare her reflection in this mirror with the standard of beauty that was provided by the bas-relief on its back. Such mirror-back images were called emblemata.

Jewels were a passion of the Romans, despite efforts of some emperors to restrict their purchase. The earrings shown here are made of pearls (left) and emeralds (right), both major imports from India.

A fragment of a delicate two-edged comb depicts a peacock—a Roman symbol of domestic harmony—standing before a basket filled with fruit. The comb was carved from imported elephant ivory.

the Erythraean Sea—a shipper's guide to the Red Sea, the Persian Gulf and the western Indian Ocean. In its day it must have been one of many similar guides to the sea lanes of the Empire and beyond; but today the tiny volume is unique, a lone survivor from the merchant literature of a vanished world.

Southeastward from Mussel harbor on the Egyptian coast of the Red Sea, wrote the captain, lies the land of Arabia, whose hinterland "is peopled by rascally men speaking two languages, who live in villages and nomadic camps, by whom those sailing off the middle course are plundered, and those surviving shipwrecks are taken for slaves.

"Navigation is dangerous along this whole coast of Arabia, which is without harbors, with bad anchorages, foul, inaccessible because of breakers and rocks, and terrible in every way. Therefore we hold our course down the middle of the gulf and pass on as fast as possible."

But at the narrowing of the straits that separate the Red Sea from the Indian Ocean, the *Periplus* author reported, a gentler country appeared, ruled by an Arabian King who resided in the inland city of Saphar. His port of Muza—with a sandy bottom "where the anchors hold safely"—swarmed with Arabian traders exporting myrrh and alabaster, and importing purple cloth, long-sleeved Arabian tunics, muslins, cloaks and multicolored sashes, as well as Roman copper, tin and coral.

As ships sailed out through the Red Sea straits into the Indian Ocean, curling around the shores of southwest Arabia, they came to the Hadramaut coast, the fabled incense lands—"mountainous and forbidding," wrote the captain, "wrapped in thick clouds and fog, and yielding frankincense from the trees." The "King of the Frankincense Country" lived in an inland city, and the frankincense was carried there on camels from the groves where it was harvested. "These incense-bearing trees are not of great height or thickness; they bear the frankincense sticking in drops on the bark, just as the trees among us in Egypt weep their gum. The frankincense is gathered by the King's slaves and those who are sent to this service for punishment. For these places are very unhealthy and pestilential even to those sailing along the coast; but almost always fatal to those working there, who also perish often from want of food."

Just beyond this land, the captain warned, the hostile territory of Persia began. The haunt of savage islanders—"a villainous lot, who use the Arabian language and wear girdles of palm leaves"—this no man's land extended across the mouth of the Persian Gulf. No wonder, then, that merchant captains preferred to avoid the Gulf by following the trail blazed by Hippalus, sailing directly from southwest Arabia across the Indian Ocean, to the Malabar coast in the south or to the port of Barygaza, northwest of Malabar.

The approach to Barygaza, located near the mouth of the Narbada River, was treacherous. "For there is so great force in the rush of the sea at the new moon," the captain declared, "especially during the flood tide at night, that if you begin the entrance at the moment when the waters are still, on the instant there is borne to you at the mouth of the river a noise like the cries of an army heard from afar; and very soon the sea itself comes rushing in over the shoals with a hoarse roar."

Despite its navigational drawbacks, Barygaza was a stupendously

A tragedy dramatized in stone

The earliest known artist's rendering of a nautical crisis is the vivid relief below, which was chiseled by an unknown sculptor on the coffin of a young boy who drowned in the Third Century A.D. The scene, at the mouth of Rome's harbor at Portus, is also a detailed representation of Roman sailing-ship rigs, both the common square rig and the more unusual fore-and-aft rig called a spritsail *(center vessel)*.

As shown in the carving, a square sail was attached to a horizontal spar hoisted at right angles to the hull on a mast set amidships. Sail was shortened by pulling on the vertical lines—brails—that ran down from the spar to the foot of the sail; this raised it in much the same manner as a Venetian blind. The mast of a fore-and-aft-rigged ship was

stepped farther forward than those of the square-riggers.

The event depicted in the carving—and explained in the sketch *(right)*—can be reconstructed as follows. The boy went rowing in a small boat near the harbor mouth on a windy day. In full view of onlookers, he fell or was swept overboard. Two ships, one square-rigged *(left)* and one sprit-rigged, went to his rescue. But the sprit-rigged vessel at the critical moment found itself on a collision course with a second square-rigger entering the harbor *(right)*. Though near the boy in the water, it was forced to veer sharply to avoid hitting the oncoming ship. By the time the square-rigger behind it had reached the spot where the boy was floundering, he had sunk beneath the choppy sea.

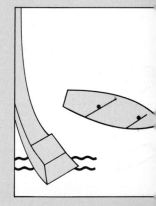

The carving shows the doomed boy amid the waves; near him is the skiff he was rowing when the waves dumped him overboard. Onlookers at left watch as a man in the bow of the ship at left crouches in a vain rescue attempt. As the ships at right jockey to avoid colliding, a sailor—assigned to trim the small bow sail of the square-rigger—evidently has panicked and is praying.

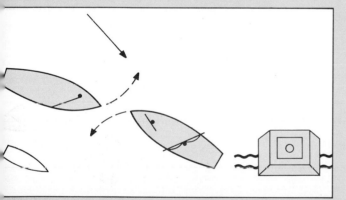

In a diagram of the rescue attempt, the two vessels at left are running before the wind. The third ship was sailing on the wind. To avoid colliding, the fore-and-aft-rigged ship turns into the wind, while the ship on the right, near the lighthouse, trims its forward sail and backs its mainsail flat to the wind, falling backward and away from the wind. The third ship holds course, but was too far away to reach the boy before he drowned.

rich port. Ivory, cotton, Chinese silk, rice—and, of course, pepper—flowed out in exchange for the coins, minerals, wine, coral, glass and other manufactured commodities of the Roman world, together with such diplomatic presents to the local King as silver dishes, harem concubines and singing boys.

Closer to the Malabar coast, the harsh shores abounded in leopards, elephants, tigers and pythons. But as merchantmen approached the far southwest of India they found the harbors and rivers filled with Arabian and Greek ships. The great port of Muziris—chief outlet for the produce of the moist, pepper-growing interior—even contained a Roman temple, and the local King's bodyguard, who watched over the city's gates and walls, was composed of fierce Western mercenaries—"the valiant-eyed Yavanas," ran a local poem, "whose bodies were strong and of terrible aspect." Here the wide-beamed merchantmen took on loads of spices, precious and semiprecious stones, fine pearls, tortoise shell and other luxury goods, and then turned back to Egypt when the northeast monsoon began to blow.

In describing the land beyond the Malabar coast, *The Periplus of the Erythraean Sea* grows cursory and confused. It touches on pearl fisheries worked by condemned criminals at the southern tip of India; the island of Ceylon, producer of muslin and jewels; and the savage eastern coast of India, land of the "Horse-faces and the Long-faces, who are said to be cannibals." It mentions the Ganges delta and "Chryse," probably the Malay Peninsula—"the last part of the inhabited world." And finally it recounts rumors of a silk-producing land lying yet farther eastward and to the north, the home of peaceable, flat-faced men. But the *Periplus* adds, "The regions beyond these places are either difficult of access because of their excessive winters and great cold, or else cannot be sought out because of some divine influence of the gods."

Here the *Periplus* ends. But as the First Century wore on, knowledge even of eastern India grew. And in about 160 A.D. a Greek mariner named Alexander crossed the Bay of Bengal, pierced the Malacca straits and touched the borders of China itself. His offer of ivory, tortoise shell and rhinoceros horn failed to impress the Chinese Emperor Huan-ti. But "from that time," recalls a Chinese chronicle, "dates the intercourse with this country." The Westerners became known and respected for their honesty; and thereafter, until trade began to fail in the Third Century, a handful of daring Western merchants trafficked directly with the Far East. Such voyages, harassed by a hundred practical perils and superstitious fears, briefly linked the two great Empires of the day—that of Rome and that of the Han Emperors of China and their successors.

Incense for Roman altars and perfumes for ladies' bosoms, silk for their robes and pearls for their toes, even animals for the Roman amphitheaters—all these imports of international trade made their contribution to the Empire's sybaritic decline. Pliny the Elder complained of a particularly egregious example—Roman ladies' infatuation with pearls from India. "Women glory in hanging these on their fingers," he wrote, "and using two or three for a single earring." They seemed to enjoy "the mere rattling together of the pearls," and they even covered their shoes with them, Pliny wrote disgustedly. The wife of one Emperor, he recounted, smothered her head, ears, neck and arms with alternating layers of emeralds and pearls, at a fabulous cost. ("She herself being ready at a moment's notice," he clucked, "to give documentary proof of her title to them.") Worse, he complained, the practice was spreading to the lower classes as well.

Pampered by such imported luxuries, Rome's magnificence sank into ruin by slow degrees. Augustus had died in 14 A.D., leaving an Empire so stable that it had survived and flourished in spite of a number of willful and extravagant Emperors, such as the deranged Caligula, who housed his horse in a stall made of marble, and even proposed that the animal be elected consul.

The Emperor Vespasian managed to restore Rome to glories resembling those of the Augustan age, and peace and prosperity returned. But by the end of the Second Century A.D., rot had set in. The debauched Emperor Commodus was strangled as a result of a palace plot, and the army took control. Soldier-emperors came and went, many of them victims of military rivalries; in one 50-year period in the Third Century there were 26 emperors, only one of whom died a natural death.

Higher taxes stifled trade. The Roman coinage was debased. Shipping firms were nationalized, and shipowners lost their incentive. Rome's navy stagnated and decayed.

Yet it was not from the sea that the inevitable invasion of the weakened Roman Empire came. Barbarians swept down from northern Europe in the Fourth Century and would twice sack Rome itself in the course of the following century. The Empire split apart. Rome and the western provinces, now occupied by Germanic tribes, fell into disarray. But in the eastern part of the Empire, the city of Constantinople, built by the Emperor Constantine on the model of Rome itself, survived as the administrative capital. Here, in the Sixth Century A.D., a fleet of war galleys was mustered once again to maintain on the sea the ancient might—and terror—of the Roman name.

The war galleys were now all two-banked vessels, fast, efficient, and armed with a new weapon called "Greek fire"—a flammable compound of naphtha, quicklime and saltpeter that was fired from catapults and primitive bronze cannon. It was the Greeks who manned the ships. And now the Empire that remained was culturally and ethnically more Greek than it was Roman.

So the maritime history of the Mediterranean had come full circle. The descendants of the Greek heroes who had sacked Troy and fought at Salamis were once again the strongest sea power in the Mediterranean, and were to hold that position until Constantinople fell to the Ottoman Turks in 1453, more than 1,000 years after the Roman Empire had divided. The Greeks' ancestry, in fact, was by now as mixed as any in the ancient world, and they were bound together less by blood than by common pride and tradition. Integral to that pride and tradition was the sea. Unlike the Roman, the Greek had seafaring deep in his habits of life and in his historical consciousness. Rich with change and promise, the sea was alike a symbol of his own mercurial nature and the instrument of his stupendous enterprise.

A synthesis of Greek and Roman seafaring tradition is accomplished in this Roman mosaic: Amphitrite, Greek goddess of the sea, and her husband Neptune, the Roman version of the Greek sea-god Poseidon, ride in a chariot through a dolphin-decorated sea.

Bibliography

Anderson, R. C., *Oared Fighting Ships*. Argus Books, 1976.

Auguet, Roland, *Cruelty and Civilization: The Roman Games*. London: George Allen and Unwin, 1972.

Bacon, Janet Ruth, *The Voyage of the Argonauts*. London: Methuen, 1925.

Balsdon, J.P.V.D., *Life and Leisure in Ancient Rome*. London: The Bodley Head, 1969.

Banca Toscana, ed., *Paintings by Allesandro Allori in the Palazzo Salviati da Cepperello*. Florence: Zincografica Fiorentina, 1953.

Bass, George F., ed., *A History of Seafaring Based on Underwater Archaeology*. Walker, 1972.

Bowra, C. M., and the Editors of Time-Life Books, *Classical Greece* (Great Ages of Man series). Time-Life Books, 1975.

Burn, Andrew Robert, *Persia and the Greeks: the Defence of the West, c. 546-478 B.C.* St. Martin's Press, 1962.

Bury, J. B. and Russell Meiggs, *A History of Greece to the Death of Alexander the Great*. St. Martin's Press, 1975.

The Cambridge Ancient History:
Vol. 5: *Athens 478-401 B.C.* Cambridge: Cambridge University Press, 1935.
Vol. 7: *The Hellenistic Monarchies and the Rise of Rome*. Cambridge: Cambridge University Press, 1934.
Vol. 10: *The Augustan Empire 44 B.C.-A.D. 70*. Macmillan, 1934.

Carcopino, Jerome, *Daily Life in Ancient Rome: the People and the City at the Height of the Empire*. Transl. by E. O. Lorimer. Yale University Press, 1940.

Carter, John M., *The Battle of Actium*. London: Hamish Hamilton, 1970.

Cary, Max and E. H. Warmington, *The Ancient Explorers*. London: Methuen, 1929.

Cary, Max and H. H. Scullard, *History of Rome Down to the Reign of Constantine*. St. Martin's Press, 1975.

Casson, Lionel, and the Editors of Time-Life Books, *Ancient Egypt* (Great Ages of Man series). Time-Life Books, 1965.

Casson, Lionel:
The Ancient Mariners: Seafarers and Sea Fighters of the Mediterranean in Ancient Times. Macmillan, 1968.
The Horizon Book of Daily Life in Ancient Rome. American Heritage, 1975.
Ships and Seamanship in the Ancient World. Princeton University Press, 1971.

Charlesworth, M. P., *Trade Routes and Commerce of the Roman Empire*. Cambridge: Cambridge University Press, 1924.

Devambez, Pierre, Robert Flacelière and

Pierre-Maxime Schuhl, *A Dictionary of Ancient Greek Civilization*. London: Methuen, 1967.

Dio Cassius, *Dio's Roman History*, Vol. 5. Transl. by Earnest Cary. Harvard University Press, 1955.

Edey, Maitland A., and the Editors of Time-Life Books, *Lost World of the Aegean* (The Emergence of Man series). Time-Life Books, 1975.

Fraser, P. M., *Ptolemaic Alexandria*. Oxford: Oxford University Press, 1972.

Grant, Michael:
The Ancient Mediterranean. Charles Scribner's Sons, 1969.
Cleopatra. London: Weidenfeld and Nicolson, 1972.
History of Rome. London: Weidenfeld and Nicolson, 1978.
Myths of the Greeks and Romans. World Publishing, 1962.
Greece and Rome. National Geographic Society, 1968.

Green, Peter:
Alexander the Great. Praeger, 1970.
The Year of Salamis 480-479 B.C. London: Weidenfeld and Nicolson, 1970.

Hadas, Moses and the Editors of Time-Life Books, *Imperial Rome* (Great Ages of Man series), Time-Life Books, 1965.

Hammond, N.G.L., *A History of Greece to 322 B.C.* Oxford: Clarendon Press, 1967.

Herodotus, *The History of Herodotus*. Vol. 2. Ed. by E. H. Blakeney. Transl. by George Rawlinson. London: J. M. Dent & Sons, 1942.

Heyerdahl, Thor, *Early Man and the Ocean*. London: George Allen and Unwin, 1978.

Hignett, C., *Xerxes' Invasion of Greece*. Oxford: Clarendon Press, 1963.

Homer, *The Odyssey*. Transl. by E. V. Rieu. Penguin Books, 1946.

Hopper, R. F., *The Early Greeks*. London: Weidenfeld and Nicolson, 1976.

Hyde, Walter Woodburn, *Ancient Greek Mariners*. Oxford University Press, 1947.

Jenkins, Nancy, *The Boat beneath the Pyramid King Cheops Royal Ship*. London: Thames and Hudson, 1980.

Johnson, Mary, *Roman Life*. Scott, Foresman, 1957.

Jones, Arnold Hugh Martin, *The Later Roman Empire, a Social, Economic and Administrative Survey*. Vol. 2. University of Oklahoma Press, 1964.

Kitto, Humphrey D. F., *The Greeks*. Penguin Books, 1965.

McCrindle, John Watson, ed., *The Commerce and Navigation of the Erythraean Sea*. Reprint, Amsterdam: Philo Press, 1973. (Originally published Editions Calcutta-London, 1879.)

Meiggs, Russell:
The Athenian Empire. Oxford: Clarendon Press, 1972.
Roman Ostia. Oxford: Clarendon Press, 1973.

Moore, Frank Gardner, *The Roman's World*. Columbia University Press, 1936.

Morrison, J. S. and R. T. Williams, *Greek Oared Ships 900-322 B.C.* Cambridge: Cambridge University Press, 1968.

Ormerod, Henry A., *Piracy in the Ancient World; an Essay in Mediterranean History*. Liverpool: The University Press of Liverpool, 1924.

The Periplus of the Erythraean Sea: Travel and Trade in the Indian Ocean by a Merchant of the First Century. Transl. by Wilfred H. Schoff, London, Bombay and Calcutta: Longmans, Green, 1912.

Perowne, Stewart, *Death of the Roman Republic from 146 B.C. to the Birth of the Roman Empire*. Doubleday, 1968.

Pliny the Elder, *Natural History*, Vols. 3 and 4. Transl. by H. Rackham. Harvard University Press, 1945.

Pliny the Younger, *Letters and Panegyricus*, Vol. 1. Transl. by Betty Radice. Harvard University Press, 1964.

Plutarch, *Plutarch's Lives*, Vols. 2 and 9. Transl. by Bernadotte Perrin. Harvard University Press, 1948.

Polybius, *The Histories of Polybius*, Vol. 1. Transl. by Evelyn S. Shuckburgh. London: Macmillan, 1889.

Rodgers, William Ledyard, *Greek and Roman Naval Warfare*. United States Naval Institute, 1937.

Rostovtzeff, M., *Rome*. Transl. by J. D. Duff. Oxford University Press, 1960.
Roe Social and Economic History of the Hellenistic World. Oxford: Clarendon Press, 1941.
The Social and Economic History of the Roman Empire. Oxford: Clarendon Press, 1957.

Sandars, N. K., *The Sea Peoples: Warriors of the Ancient Mediterranean 1250-1150 B.C.* London: Thames and Hudson, 1978.

Simnigen, William G. and Arthur E. R. Book, *A History of Ancient Rome to A.D. 565*. Macmillan, 1977.

Snodgrass, Anthony M., *Arms and Armour of the Greeks*. Cornell University Press, 1967.

Starr, Chester G., *The Roman Imperial Navy 31 B.C.-324 A.D.* Cornell University Press, 1941.

Strabo, *The Geography of Strabo*, Vol. 8. Transl. by Horace Leonard Jones. London: William Heinemann, 1930.

Tacitus, *The Annals*, Vol. 2. Transl. by John Jackson. Harvard University Press,

1962.
Suetonius, *The Twelve Caesars*. Transl. by Robert Graves. Penguin Books, 1957.
Thiel, J. H.:
A History of Roman Sea Power before the Second Punic War. North-Holland Publishing, 1954.
Studies on the History of Roman Sea Power in Republican Times. North-Holland Publishing, 1946.

Van der Heyden, A.A.M. and H. H. Scullard, *Atlas of the Classical World*. London: Nelson, 1960.
Wallinga, H. T., *The Boarding Bridge of the Romans: Its Construction and Its Function in the Naval Tactics of the First Punic War*. J. B. Walters, 1956.
Warmington, E. H., *The Commerce between the Roman Empire and India*. Cambridge: Cambridge University Press, 1928.

Warren, Peter, *The Aegean Civilizations*. E. P. Dutton, 1975.
Wheeler, Sir Mortimer, *Rome beyond the Imperial Frontiers*. Greenwood Press, 1971.
Zimmern, Alfred, *The Greek Commonwealth. Politics and Economics in Fifth Century Athens*. The Modern Library, 1956.

Picture Credits

The sources for the illustrations in this book are shown below. Credits for the illustrations from left to right are separated by semicolons; from top to bottom they are separated by dashes.
Cover: Scala, courtesy Musei Vaticani, Rome. Front and back endpapers: Drawing by Peter McGinn.
Page 3: Courtesy of the Trustees of the British Museum, London. 6, 7: Courtesy of The Oriental Institute, University of Chicago. 10, 11: Ekdotiki Athenon, Athens. 13-16: from *The Boat Beneath the Pyramid* by Nancy Jenkins with photographs by John Ross, published by Thames and Hudson Ltd., and Holt, Rinehart & Winston Inc., New York, 1980. 18, 19: Courtesy of the Trustees of the British Museum, London. 20, 21: Scala, courtesy Musée du Louvre, Paris. 22: Erich Lessing, courtesy Bibliothèque Nationale, Paris. 23: Istituto Archeologico Germanico, Rome, courtesy Museo Archeologico Nazionale, Sperlonga. 24, 25: Scala, courtesy Museo Nazionale Tarquinese, Tarquinia—Musée du Louvre, Paris; from *A Fantastic Bestiary—Beasts and Monsters in Myth and Folklore* by Ernst and Johann Lehner, published by Tudor Publishing Co., New York, 1969; from *The Gods of the Greeks* by C. Kerenyi, published by Thames and Hudson Ltd., London, 1951—David Lees, courtesy Museo Nazionale, Tarento. 27: Alinari-Giraudon, courtesy Villa Albani, Rome. 28, 29: Alinari, courtesy Musei Vaticani, Rome. 30: Alinari-Giraudon, courtesy Musée du Louvre, Paris. 32-39: Erich Lessing, courtesy Banca Toscana Palace, Florence. 40, 41: München Foto Blauel, courtesy Bayerische Staatsgemäldesommlungen, Munich. 43: Courtesy of The Oriental Institute, University of Chicago. 45, 47: Drawing by Nicholas Fasciano. 48, 49: Ekdotiki Athenon, Athens. 50-54: Drawings by Nicholas Fasciano. 56, 57: Drawing by Victor Lazzaro,

Map by Nicholas Fasciano. 58, 59: Melissa Publications, Athens, courtesy National Gallery of Athens. 60, 61: Courtesy Antikenmuseum, Staatliche Museen Preussischer Kulturbesitz, Berlin (West); Courtesy of the Trustees of the British Museum, London; Erich Lessing, courtesy Archeological Museum, Sofia. 62, 63: The Metropolitan Museum of Art, Dick Fund, 1954. 64, 65: Henry Groskinsky, courtesy Soprintendenza Archeologica di Ostia, Rome; Ekdotiki Athenon, Athens; Erich Lessing, courtesy Archeological Museum, Athens; Erich Lessing, courtesy Kunsthistorisches Museum, Vienna; Epigraphic Museum, Athens. 68-73: Drawings by John Batchelor. 74: Photo Bibliothèque Nationale, Paris. 77: Map by Nicholas Fasciano. 78: Alinari, courtesy Musei Vaticani, Rome. 80, 81: Drawing by Richard Schlecht, based on research by J. Richard Steffy; Michale L. Katzev, courtesy Kyrenia Ship Project, Athens. 83: Courtesy of the Trustees of the British Museum, London. 86: Spyros Tsavdaroglou, Athens, courtesy Professor Manolis Andronikos, Salonika. 87: Ny Carlsberg Glyptotek, Copenhagen. 89: Courtesy of the Trustees of the British Museum, London. 90, 91: Photo Hachette, courtesy Collection Mobilier National, Paris. 92-97: Renderings by Victor Lazzaro, based on original research and drawings by John Taktikos, except map, page 95, by Nicholas Fasciano. 98: Courtesy of the Trustees of the British Museum, London. 101: from *Histoire de Polybe*, translated by Vincent Thuillier, published by Chez Arkstée and Merkus, Amsterdam, 1774. 103: Anderson, courtesy Musei Capitolini, Rome. 106, 107: Drawings by Nicholas Fasciano, based on research by G. Kelly Tipps. 109: Istituto Archeologico Germanico, Rome. 110, 111: Scala, courtesy Soprintendenza alle Antichità della Campania, Naples. 115: Map by Nicholas Fasciano—Alinari, courtesy Mu-

seo Archeologico Nazionale, Naples. 118, 119: Roger Wood, courtesy of the Trustees of the British Museum, London; Courtesy of the Trustees of the British Museum, London; Alinari-Giraudon, courtesy Musei Vaticani, Rome. 120, 121: Derek Bayes, courtesy National Maritime Museum, London. 122: Courtesy of the Trustees of the British Museum, London. 125-128: Patrimonio Nacional, Madrid. 130, 131: Collezione Torlonia, Rome. 133: Istituto Archeologico Germanico, courtesy Museo Nazionale d'Antichità, Ravenna. 134, 135: Map by Nicholas Fasciano. 136, 137: Courtesy Stephen Natanson. 139: Kevin Berry, courtesy Musée des Augustins, Toulouse. 140-144: Erich Lessing, courtesy Soprintendenza alle Antichità, Agrigento. 147: Drawings by Nicholas Fasciano. 148, 149: Anderson, courtesy Musei Vaticani, Rome. 150, 151: Musei Vaticani, Rome. 152, 153: Soprintendenza Archeologica di Ostia, Rome. 154: Alinari-Giraudon, courtesy Torlonia Museum, Rome. 156, 157: Drawing by Victor Lazzaro. 158: Drawing by Nicholas Fasciano. 159: Soprintendenza Archeologica di Ostia, Rome. 161: Henry Groskinsky, courtesy Museo Archeologico Nazionale, Naples—Scala, courtesy Museo Archeologico Nazionale, Naples. 162, 163: Scala, courtesy Museo Archeologico Nazionale, Naples—Henry Groskinsky, courtesy Museo Archeologico Nazionale, Naples; Scala, courtesy Museo Archeologico Nazionale, Naples; Henry Groskinsky, courtesy Museo Archeologico Nazionale, Naples—Scala, courtesy Museo Archeologico Nazionale, Naples. 164: Henry Groskinsky, courtesy Museo Archeologico Nazionale, Naples. 166, 167: from *The Ancient Mariners* by Lionel Casson, The Macmillan Co., New York, 1967—Alinari, courtesy Ny Carlsberg Glyptotek, Copenhagen. 169: Giraudon, courtesy Musée du Louvre, Paris.

Acknowledgments

The index for this book was prepared by Gale Linck Partoyan. The editors wish to thank the following artists: John Batchelor, Nicholas Fasciano, Victor Lazzaro, Peter McGinn and Richard Schlecht.

The editors also wish to thank: In Austria: Vienna—Dr. Georg Kugler, Dr. Wolfgang Oberleitner, Kunsthistorisches Museum. In France: Paris—Marjolaine Mathikine, Director for Historical Studies, Claude Bellarbre, Jacques Chantriot, Catherine Touny, Musée de la Marine; Jean Coural, Director, Mobilier National; Marie Montembault, Brigitte Tailliez, Département des Antiquités Grecques et Romaines, Musée du Louvre; Toulouse—Denis Milhau, Curator, Musée des Augustins. In Greece: Athens—Michael Katzev, Kyrenia Ship Project. In Italy: Agrigento—Professor Ernesto de Miro, Superintendent, Graziella Fiorentini, Soprintendenza alle Antichità; Florence—On. Marino Bardotti, Director, Primo Fabbri, Banca Toscana; Naples—Enrica Pozzi-Paolini, Muséo Archeologico Nazionale; Profesor Fausto Zevi, Superintendent, Renata Cantilena, Soprintendenza alle Antichità della Compania; Piazza Armerina—Giovanni Anzaldi, Villa Romana del Casale; Rome—Valnea Santamaria Scrinari, Superintendent, Giuseppina Lauro, Soprintendenza alle Antichità di Ostia; Amministrazione Torlonia; Direzione Musei Vaticani; Taranto—Ettore de Juliis, Superintendent, Giuseppe Andreazzi, Soprintendenza Archeologica della Puglia. In Spain: Madrid—Paulina Junquera. In the United Kingdom: Cambridge—J. S. Morrison; London—A. Finnimore, Dr. D. Williams, Ray Gardner, Department of Greek and Roman Antiquities, British Museum; Honor Frost.

The editors also wish to thank: In the United States: Chicago, Illinois—John A. Larson, Archivist, Photographic Services, The Oriental Institute; College Station, Texas—Professor G. Richard Steffy, Institute of Nautical Archaeology, Texas A&M University; New York, New York—Stacy Aronowitz; Dr. Robert Bianchi, Associate Curator, Egyptian and Classical Art, The Brooklyn Museum; Mathilde Camacho, Newsweek Magazine; Deanna Cross, Mary F. Doherty, Photograph Library, The Metropolitan Museum of Art; Dora Petrizi Jones; Sotiris Mousouris; Sergio Nichele; Charles Osborne; John E. Taktikos; Lyn Yonack, Tudor Publishing Company; Lydia Zelaya, The Macmillan Company; Old Greenwich, Connecticut—Perrot Library; Tampa, Florida—Professor G. Kelly Tipps, University of South Florida.

Particularly valuable sources of quotations were *The Ancient Mariners: Seafarers and Sea Fighters of the Mediterranean in Ancient Times* by Lionel Casson, Macmillan, 1968; *The History of Herodotus*, Vol. 2 by Herodotus, edited by E. H. Blakeney, translated by George Rawlinson, London: J. M. Dent & Sons, 1942; *The Commerce and Navigation of the Erythraean Sea* edited by John Watson McCrindle, Amsterdam: Philo Press, 1973 (Originally published Editions Calcutta-London, 1879); *The Periplus of the Erythraean Sea: Travel and Trade in the Indian Ocean by a Merchant of the First Century*, translated by Wilfred H. Schoff, London, Bombay, and Calcutta: Longmans, Green, 1912; *The Histories of Polybius*, Vol. 1 by Polybius, translated by Evelyn S. Shuckburgh, London: Macmillan, 1889.

Index

Printed in U.S.A.

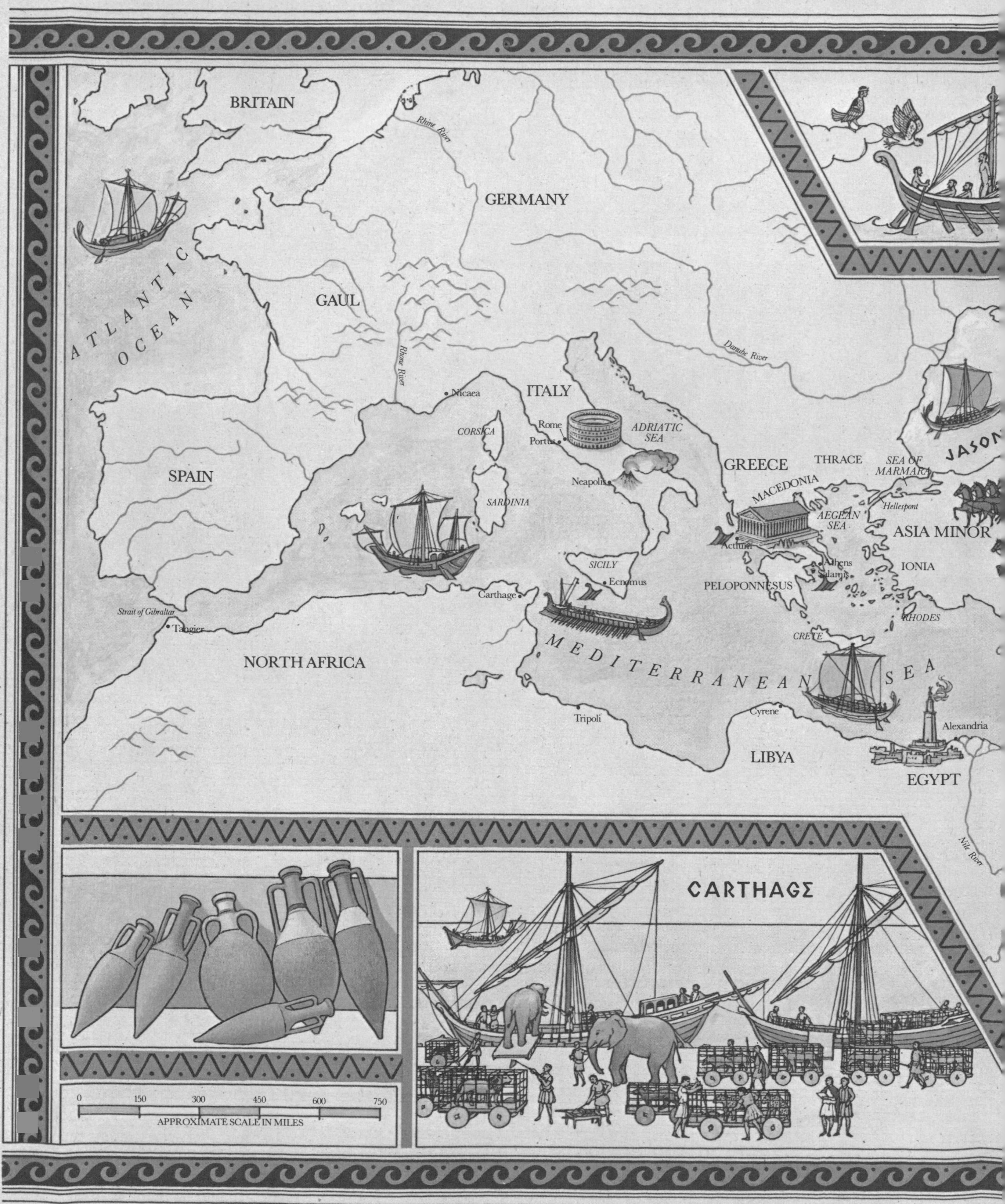

BRITAIN

Rhine River

GERMANY

ATLANTIC
OCEAN

GAUL

Rhone River

Danube River

ITALY

Nicaea

CORSICA

Rome
Portus

ADRIATIC
SEA

SPAIN

SARDINIA

Neapolis

GREECE   THRACE   *SEA OF
MARMARA*

JASON

MACEDONIA

Hellespont

*AEGEAN
SEA*

ASIA MINOR

Actium

SICILY

Athens
Salamis

IONIA

Ecnomus

PELOPONNESUS

RHODES

Carthage

CRETE

Strait of Gibraltar

Tangier

NORTH AFRICA

M E D I T E R R A N E A N   S E A

Tripoli

Cyrene

Alexandria

LIBYA

EGYPT

Nile River

CARTHAGE